The Northern Horizons of Guy Blanchet

Intrepid Surveyor, 1884–1966

D1736934

The Northern Horizons of Guy Blanchet

Intrepid Surveyor, 1884–1966

Gwyneth Hoyle

NATURAL HERITAGE BOOKS
A MEMBER OF THE DUNDURN GROUP
TORONTO

Published by Natural Heritage Books	Gazelle Book Services Limited	Dundurn Press
A Member of the Dundurn Group	White Cross Mills	2250 Military Road
3 Church Street, Suite 500	High Town, Lancaster, England	Tonawanda, NY
Toronto, Ontario, M5E 1M2, Canada	LA1 4XS	U.S.A 14150

Edited by Jane Gibson
Designed by Erin Mallory

Printed and bound in Canada by Marquis
www.dundurn.com

Library and Archives Canada Cataloguing in Publication

Hoyle, Gwyneth
    The northern horizons of Guy Blanchet : intrepid
surveyor, 1884-1966 / Gwyneth Hoyle.

Includes index.
ISBN 978-1-55002-759-4

    1. Blanchet, Guy Houghton, 1884-1966. 2. Canada, Northern--Biography. 3. Surveyors--Canada--Biography. I. Title.

TA533.B53H69 2007   526.9'092   C2007-904654-1

1   2   3   4   5   11   10   09   08   07

Front cover: "Guy Blanchet and cairn at the beginning of Coppermine River, 1924."
    Courtesy of Janet Blanchet

We acknowledge the support of the **Canada Council for the Arts** and the **Ontario Arts Council** for our publishing program. We also acknowledge the financial support of the **Government of Canada** through the **Book Publishing Industry Development Program** and **The Association for the Export of Canadian Books**, and the **Government of Ontario** through the **Ontario Book Publishers Tax Credit** program and the **Ontario Media Development Corporation**.

J. Kirk Howard, President

Table of Contents

Acknowledgements

I would like to acknowledge the use of material from the following sources:

Archives, Canadian Imperial Bank of Commerce
British Columbia Archives
Dartmouth College Library, Hanover, New Hampshire
Glenbow Institute, Calgary
National Archives of Canada
Trent University Archives
The Beaver

To James Raffan, writer and northern traveller, go my profound thanks for taking time away from his own writing to read my first draft and give me his carefully written, insightful comments, and the benefit of his wide experience.

Preface

Over a lifetime of reading accounts of northern travel, I found the name of Guy Blanchet becoming familiar to me from his articles in *The Beaver* and his book, *Search in the North*. On learning that his papers were held in the British Columbia Archives, I made a brief exploratory visit there several years ago. In one of his diaries, written in 1924, I was intrigued by the statement, "It feels strange to think that this may be my last long trip in the North." In fact, his travels in the North continued for the rest of his working life — about twenty more years. The North had laid its spell on him, and he continued to work and travel there in all seasons and conditions, using every available means of transportation from dog teams to airplanes.

A few years after my first visit to the archives, at the annual gathering of wilderness travellers in Toronto, one of the speakers was Janet Blanchet. She gave a presentation about her father, R.M. Patterson, the man whose book *Dangerous River* introduced the fabulous valley of the Nahanni to the reading public. While I had read and enjoyed all of Patterson's books, my question to her was, "Do you have any connection to Guy Blanchet?" and her reply, "He was my husband's uncle," both surprised and delighted me. Throughout the writing of this biography, Janet has always been ready to answer my questions, and suggest other persons I might contact.

Among those contacts, is Cathleen Converse-Kess who is currently writing the biography of Muriel Wylie Blanchet (otherwise known as Capi), Janet's mother-in-law, and she and I have been able to exchange much useful information about the Blanchet family. Janet also put me in touch with her nephew, Richard Guy Blanchet, the custodian of many of Guy Blanchet's photographs, which he has generously loaned to illustrate this book.

During the short weeks spent at the archives in Victoria, I have appreciated the hospitality of Suzanne Hamilton and Dorothy Grieve, who also retrieved essential archival material that I had overlooked during my concentrated reading there. In Peterborough, Kathy Hooke, the niece of George Douglas, and Enid Mallory, author of *Coppermine*, gave me copies of correspondence between Douglas and Blanchet. Knowing of my interest in the subject, Prof. R.H. Cockburn, of Fredericton, sent me some discarded correspondence files from the Department of Energy, Mines and Resources, which provided insights into the workings of the Survey Office in Ottawa.

Professor Suzanne Bailey of the English Department at Trent University, who teaches a course in the Literature of Travel, has encouraged me by reading and discussing chapters as they were written, as has my husband, Alex. Bob Parr, retired partner in the surveying company of Elliott and Parr, explained some of the technicalities of the profession and commented on my descriptions of it. Michael Peake used his skill and knowledge of the North to scan the photographs from Blanchet's albums. Thanks also to Douglas Hoyle who was always available to guide me through computer problems.

Introduction

The beginnings of cartography are lost in the mists of time. Early man drew maps on the walls of caves, in the sand or on dried animal skins to show where to find game, water in the desert, or even to tell those coming behind where the leaders of the tribe had gone. The ancient Babylonians, discovering that the sun and stars followed a regular path in the heavens, compiled a catalogue of their movements and produced the idea of dividing the sun's path into the twelve signs of the zodiac, which gradually evolved into 360 degrees, with further sub-divisions into minutes and seconds. Egyptians under the Pharaohs, and later the Greeks, made use of this knowledge to create maps that bore some resemblance to the maps of today. Cartography had become a science, making surveying one of the oldest professions in the world.[1]

Surveyors are known to have been part of the work force that built the pyramids of ancient Egypt, using their skill to mark the positions of the sites and directing the labourers and slaves to move the huge stone blocks to the correct locations. The pharaohs employed them to lay out plots of land along the Nile and those early surveyors made their measurements using knotted rope, stretched and soaked in beeswax to maintain its integrity.[2] On Egyptian hieroglyphics there are representations of men using instruments to take sightings of the sun or stars to locate a geographical position.

The work of modern surveyors is all around us. Highways, city streets, railways and airport runways could not have been built without them. Maps, boundaries, mining claims, property title deeds, even skyscrapers, require their skill and variety of techniques. Aeroplanes, cameras, computers, satellites and electronic measuring devices have changed the way they work, and only increase our admiration for the perseverance, stamina and accuracy of those who mapped and measured this country using Gunter's chain or metal tape, transits, rods and wooden pickets before such sophisticated equipment had been invented.

The life and work of Guy Blanchet, one of the pre-eminent surveyors of the first half of the twentieth century, gives a colourful picture of the rugged, physical challenges that the men working in northern areas of Canada accepted and even enjoyed as part of their job. In the various books on the history of surveying in Canada, he is one of the handful singled out from thousands of practising surveyors for the precision, thoroughness and extent of his work. In telling his story, I am paying tribute to the pioneer members of this profession, who are among the unsung heroes of this country.

List of Maps

Prologue

The year is 1906. A young man is striding east across the prairie following a cart track. As he walks, he peers into the distant horizon and occasionally glances at a piece of paper containing rough directions. The land, nearly flat, seems to be made of a series of broad pie plates, and as he climbs each rim his gaze sweeps in all directions. He is looking for a survey party, which, he was told, was in need of an assistant. In his pocket is a letter of introduction from an Edmonton surveyor. The man is Guy Blanchet.

He had come south from Edmonton on the train to Lacombe and taken the branch line to the village of Stettler at the "end of steel." Leaving his bag at the little country hotel, he asked about a government survey working in the area. The proprietor said, "Yes, — somewhere out there," and pointed to the east.

The sun beat down on the open prairie, and late in the afternoon Guy was glad to arrive at a pioneering ranch. The farmer, struggling to plough a fire guard around his stacks of wheat with oxen untrained for the job, gave him an hospitable welcome, a good meal and a bed for the night.

First thing in the morning, he set off again following the same track, which was becoming fainter and fainter. After walking thirty miles he arrived at the homestead of a young Englishman who had a sod house, a team of horses and little else. Glad of company the young man gave him a frugal meal, and they slept under horse blankets with sand trickling down from the sod roof, probably disturbed by mice. The man, having heard nothing of a survey party, advised him to return to the town of Red Deer, and pointed out the track to follow.

The track ended at the Red Deer River but could be seen emerging on the other side. Having been told it could be forded by horses, Guy had no choice but to wade into the swift current, waist-deep and flowing over slippery boulders. He emerged on the far side with a sense of accomplishment, and his dripping clothes gradually dried in the sun. After another night at a friendly ranch, he set off for Red Deer where he knew of a family that had come from Ottawa, his home town. Over a welcome dinner, he told them his story and they urged him to hurry and catch the train back to Edmonton — not realizing that he had no money to buy a ticket.

Knowing that he could walk about three-and-a-half miles an hour, Guy reckoned he could follow the railway track the eighty miles to Edmonton in three days, although food might be a problem. Passing a farmer's field he dug a few turnips to munch, and after a passenger train went by he came upon a bonanza of chicken bones thrown from the dining car. The afternoon was dragging on interminably, when a passing freight train slowed down to climb a grade. As it went by the engineer signalled to him to climb aboard. Guy missed on the first try, landing in a ditch, but it was a long, slow train and on his second attempt he made it and climbed to the roof of a freight car.

At the next station, a brakeman spotted him on the roof and told him he couldn't travel there, but added gruffly, "Get aboard." Guy found a half-empty coal car and settled into a corner where he was not seen by the inspectors at the stations where they stopped. About midnight they reached the rail yard at Strathcona, and Guy emerged covered with coal dust, giving the railway policeman the excuse that he was just coming off shift. He found a fourth rate hotel in Strathcona where the night clerk let him sleep in the lobby and wash in the basement in the morning.

Still dishevelled, his clothes bearing the testimony of his travels, Guy presented himself first thing in the morning at the office of Alfred Driscoll, the surveyor who had sent him on the wild-goose chase. Guy had been more than halfway across Alberta, covering an elliptical area of several hundred square miles in his search for the elusive survey party. If Driscoll had been testing him to see if he had the perseverance, stamina and imagination for the life of a surveyor, he was satisfied by the result. He offered Guy a temporary job within the City of Edmonton to tide him over until he could find work with a Government survey and, seeing Guy's somewhat destitute condition, gave him a small advance of money, just enough to secure his lodging in the Riverside House in Edmonton and send to Stettler for his luggage.[1]

This was the beginning of a career that would eventually take Guy deep into the wilderness, allow him to explore large areas of the North, and satisfy his lifelong need for adventure.

ONE — EARLY LIFE: 1884–1906

Guy Blanchet had roots that reached back to the earliest French settlement, and was as intrinsically Canadian as the Precambrian Shield, the geographical feature where he spent much of his working life. In his profession as a surveyor, the land provided his livelihood while at the same time it nourished his spirit. In his work of mapping and exploration in the North, he often followed the traditional paths of the First Nations People and whenever possible they were his preferred guides and companions. Had he been born in an earlier century he might have been a coureur de bois ranging over vast tracts of unexplored country, and coming home with tales to tell. Even in the twentieth century his work covered large swaths of the North, and always he returned home with stories.

Those stories were sometimes published in journals such as *The Beaver, The Canadian Field-Naturalist,* the *Bulletin of the Geographical Society of Philadelphia* and columns in the weekend edition of the Victoria newspaper, *The Daily Colonist.* His eighteen-month-long stint in charge of the base camp on the coast of Hudson Bay for a mining company involved in aerial prospecting was the source of material for Blanchet's one book, *Search in the North.* Many of his experiences were only recorded in personal journals written during survey and other trips, and are housed in the Provincial Archives of British Columbia in Victoria. Also in that archive is the manuscript, written late in life, containing details of his childhood and stories from his early years as a surveyor.

Guy Houghton Blanchet was born in Ottawa in 1884, only a generation after Queen Victoria had decreed in 1858 that the brawling lumber and sawmill town of Bytown, at the confluence of the Ottawa and Rideau rivers, would change its name to Ottawa and become the designated capital of the Province of Canada. The Gothic stone building of the new parliament, completed just before Confederation in 1867 stood proudly on the hill above the river, looking down over the growing city. The fine stone house of one of Bytown's most successful pioneers was converted to be the temporary viceregal residence for the Queen's representative, where it remains with considerable improvements and additions as the Rideau Hall of today. Despite these handsome buildings, Ottawa was not far removed from the backwoods and the frontier, with many ugly buildings and dirty streets. As the Honourable Wilfrid Laurier remarked in the year that Guy Blanchet was born, "Ottawa is not a handsome city and does not appear to be destined to become one either."[1]

Guy was ninth of the eleven children of Ludger Blanchet, a Canadian proud of being able to trace his ancestry back to one of the original French settlers in Canada, and Mary Amelia Hunton, the daughter of a pioneer English merchant in Bytown. Their children were brought up speaking English and had names that were mostly interchangeable in English or French, such as Herbert, Paul, Arthur, Florence and Helen. Guy's name was always pronounced in the English way, to rhyme with "Why."[2]

The Blanchet family in North America, numerous and widely dispersed over the continent, all claim a common ancestor in Pierre Blanchet, who was born in 1642 at St. Omer-de-Rosieres, not far from Calais, France. He sailed to New France in 1666, was recorded in the census of 1667, and on February 17, 1670, he married Marie Fournier,[3] the great-granddaughter of Louis Hébert, thus linking him to one of the earliest settlers in the new colony.

Louis Hébert, recognized as the first Canadian settler to support himself by tilling the soil, was connected by marriage to Jean de Biencourt de Poutrincourt,[4] sailed with Champlain and de Poutrincourt to the New World in 1606 and wintered at Port-Royal, in what is now Nova Scotia, before the expedition was recalled to France. Determined to settle in the New World, Hébert made another voyage in 1610 and again in 1617 he returned to the St. Lawrence with Champlain, this time bringing along his wife and three children. Skilled as an apothecary who treated both the members of the fur-trading community and the Native people, he was granted one of the first seigneuries in Canada, Sault-au-Matelot, part of present-day Québec City. There, until his death in 1627, Hébert grew vegetables and grain, pastured cattle and cultivated an orchard planted with apple trees brought from Normandy.[5]

The original Pierre Blanchet was a farmer and a weaver who, with his wife, Marie, took up land on the south shore of the St. Lawrence at St. Pierre-de-la-Rivière-du-Sud, near the present-day town of Montmagny, and raised a family of fifteen children. Guy's father, Ludger, fifth generation from Pierre, was born in St. Gervais, in the Bellechasse region south of Québec City, and was a notary public who rose in his profession to be a judge of the Québec Court of Appeal. Ludger, born in 1839, left Québec for an appointment in the civil service in Ottawa. He arrived there on April 27, 1867, just before Confederation, to take up a position in the accounting section of the Post Office department, one of the largest departments of the government, in which nearly a quarter of the 280 civil servants were employed.[6]

As he walked to his office in the West Block of the Parliament building, Ludger Blanchet often passed the dry goods store of T. & W. Hunton, on Sparks Street, with its attractive display of imported silks and shawls, clothing and hats. Thomas Hunton and his brother William from England were among the early commercial pioneers in Bytown. Not only did they sell clothing they manufactured on the premises, but also carpets, blankets and most of the dry goods needed to furnish a house, all spelled out in a full column advertisement each day on the back page of the *Ottawa Citizen*. Thomas Hunton lived above the business on Sparks Street[7] and in 1867 his sixteen-year-old daughter, Mary Amelia, was old enough to serve behind the counter in the store, where it is possible that she caught the eye of Ludger Blanchet. On January 23 of the following year she and Ludger were married.

By 1875, the *Ottawa City Directory* shows that Ludger and Mary were raising a family on King Street, renamed King Edward Street when Edward VII ascended the throne. Ludger had a secure

Courtesy of Janet Blanchet

Ludger Blanchet and Mary Hunton, about the time of their marriage, 1868, photographed in the Topley Studio of Ottawa, the official viceregal photographer.

position with a stable income in the Post Office Department, rising gradually from being a 2nd class clerk to near the top of the 1st class. Ludger Blanchet was also skilled at drawing and earned extra income by illustrating events for the Ottawa newspapers.[8] After a few years he was able to move his growing family across the canal to #117 Cooper Street, a neighbourhood where many senior civil servants had their homes. It seems likely that the Blanchet family did not own their home because several years later, they moved one block south to Somerset Street, first to #126 and a year later, to #152. They would have needed a large house because in 1897, when Guy was thirteen, all eleven children were still living at home with their parents, where Geraldine, the oldest of the family, gave piano lessons. It was an easy walk for the three oldest boys to their work as clerks in various commercial businesses nearby. In 1900 the newly arrived civil servant, Mackenzie King, living in lodgings on Somerset Street, thought Ottawa a very dull place.[9]

Many years later Guy recalled a happy childhood in the area around #117 Cooper Street when life was simple but satisfactory, money was scarce but prices were low. Their meals were nourishing but plain, porridge for breakfast, and dinner at noon always ended with a freshly baked cake cut into thirteen pieces, except on birthdays when the guest of honour was given two pieces. The children amused themselves with games such as marbles and tops, and in the outdoors there was swimming, boating on the canal in summer, and snowshoeing and skating in winter. They made camps in the holidays as far away as Hog's Back Bay where a few pine trees had been preserved, or they used their boat to go down the canal to picnic below the first lock at Munsey's Bridge.[10] In the summer they sometimes went to a farm near Fairy Lake, and later the family went farther afield to the lake at Kingsmere in the Gatineau hills. Guy's father enjoyed leading his brood on walks at the end of the day, around Parliament Hill, past the gargoyle that discharged cold water into a tin cup attached by a chain, or in spring they might take the dusty road from Elgin Street past farmland to gather wild strawberries, or in autumn, beechnuts. From their home it was a convenient walk for their father to reach his office, now moved to the Langevin Building on Wellington Street.

The Ottawa of Guy's childhood was far removed from the metropolitan capital city of today. People walked everywhere out of necessity, and for pleasure, a mile or two was considered no distance. There were still toll gates on the main roads leading out of the town, with a gatekeeper's house guarding them. Horses were everywhere,

Courtesy of Janet Blanchet

The Blanchet family, photo taken circa 1890. Six-year-old Guy is seated on the floor at his father's feet.

used by the milkman, the bread man, by stores making deliveries, by cabs for hire, or by the wealthy, with their high-stepping carriage teams. They even pulled the cars of the Ottawa City Passenger Railway, the round-trip route through the main streets taking seventy minutes. It was a cold ride in winter in unheated cars with straw on the floor for insulation, and a bumpy one in spring when the thawing streets developed deep potholes. Horses also pulled the two-wheeled fire wagons, each with a reel holding 500 feet of hose, which would race to find the location of the fire according to the number of bells rung at city hall. By the time Guy was born, the brigade of volunteer firefighters had been replaced by professionals, badly needed in a city with a history of serious fires.[11]

On a memorable day in late June of 1891, seven-year-old Guy had his first ride on the new electric street railway that replaced the horse-drawn cars. Despite the electric railway, the unpaved streets were a sea of mud in spring, and so thick with blowing dust in summer that the merchants on Sparks Street regularly paid to have the street sprinkled with water. The electric power from the

Chaudière Falls powered new electric street lamps that used carbon sticks, which had to be adjusted each morning. On the electric streetcars the family could take excursions to the spacious grounds of the Dominion Experimental Farm[12] for picnics in the arboretum, to beautiful Rockcliffe Park or to Britannia Beach on the Ottawa River.

Earlier in that June of 1891, Guy would have seen the funeral procession for Sir John A. Macdonald, which began at the parliament buildings, moved slowly down Elgin Street, crossed the canal bridge on Maria at the end of Albert Street to reach the little church of St. Alban the Martyr on Daly Street. As the mile-long procession began its journey, the tower bell of the Parliament building began to toll, joined by the bells of every church in the city. The Dominion police led off, preceding the black-plumed hearse, which was followed by mounted dragoon guards, military bands, coaches carrying the pallbearers and mourners, and then the lieutenant-governors of all the provinces, the judiciary, members of the Senate and of Parliament, the consular representatives, members of the civil service and many more. Ludger Blanchet took his family to join the thousands of people lining the streets along the route. It was a day of unusually oppressive heat, and with shops and houses draped in black and purple, it was a scene to impress itself on a child's memory.

Although Guy did not write about it, the great fire of 1900 was another event that was seared into the memories of everyone in Ottawa at the time. It began at a house in Hull in mid-morning of a late April day, with sparks from the chimney setting the roof ablaze. There was a strong north wind blowing and by noon the fire was out of control, destroying the centre of Hull. Flying sparks ignited the piles of lumber on both banks of the river south to the border of the Experimental Farm, destroying everything in its wake. Fortunately, the wind changed and the centre of Ottawa was saved. While Hull had been gutted, and 40% of the population made homeless, in Ottawa an area three miles long and a quarter mile wide was burned, and 2,000 homes destroyed. By the end of the day, 14,000 persons were homeless. The fire was stopped at Bronson Avenue, about ten blocks from the Blanchet home.

Guy remembered the cries of the street vendors: "Colle, colle" (coal oil), "Straw, straw" (to fill the ticking for mattresses), "Rags, bottles and bones," and the bell of the scissor grinder. As well, he remembered more musical sounds: the old man with the hand organ, the Italian man and his wife who hauled a mechanical piano through the streets, and the German band that played in the parks. In winter the air was filled with the sound of sleigh bells on the horses.

His memories are summed up in a poem by Arthur Bourinot, son of Sir John Bourinot, clerk of the House of Commons. He was a few years younger than Guy, but lived only a short distance away at #141 Cooper Street:

> And now to revert
> to those old days
> on Cooper St.
> with its wooden sidewalks
> and often rotten planks
> and the German bands
> played in the evenings
> under the corner lights...[13]

This indeed was the Ottawa of Guy Blanchet's childhood.

There was a glittering social life centred around the viceregal family, the upper echelons of parliament and the senior civil service. By contrast, the lower-ranking civil servants, to which Ludger Blanchet belonged, lived comfortable but humdrum lives in a humdrum town.

From the Blanchet home it was only a block or so to walk to Ottawa Collegiate Institute, one of the best grammar schools in the country, later renamed Lisgar Collegiate. While the four oldest children in the family appear not to have gone beyond high school, the seven younger ones all had some form of professional training.

When the time came for Guy to go to university, his choice to study mining engineering gives the first indication of where his heart lay. Of all the branches of science and engineering, mining was the one that was certain to take him away from cities into the vast, mainly unexplored Canadian hinterland. McGill University

Courtesy of BC Archives, #1-68468

Guy Blanchet, the newly graduated mining engineer, McGill, 1905.

in Montreal, within reach of Ottawa, was the oldest school for that discipline on the continent after Columbia University in New York. To the regular engineering subjects of mathematics, sciences and drawing, was added the study of metallurgy, including visits to working mines and ore-processing plants, and the school stressed the need for the students to gain practical experience during the summer.[14] The study of geology opened his eyes to the structure and form of the land, a valuable asset all his working life. Guy did well at McGill, receiving a prize for best student paper of the year in 1904,[15] and graduating in 1905, at the age of twenty-one.

Mining was at a low ebb in eastern Canada, and Guy found work as the supervising engineer of a coal mine on the Alberta side of the continental divide near Crow's Nest Pass. Founded in 1901 by two British Columbia gold prospectors, the coal mine in the foothills of the mountains was a huge success in the beginning. A spur line was built along Gold Creek from the railway at the flourishing town of Frank, to the original mining camp, known as "French Camp." This camp grew into the company town of Lille, with a school, a hospital, a hotel, a livery stable, a general store and liquor store, a bakery and a butcher shop, and, when Guy arrived there in 1905, had about 400 permanent residents. The miners, mainly single men from Britain, France, Belgium and Italy, lived in bunkhouses and rooming houses, and Guy, a young, inexperienced university graduate, far from home, found little community life there. Lille is now a ghost town and historic coal-mine site.[16]

As the supervisor of the mine at Lille, Guy spent two days a week underground, surveying and measuring the work done on the coal face. The smoky flame of the little "tea-cup" lamps fuelled by whale oil barely illuminated the dripping gloom of the passages through the mine. The open flame was a constant danger in the air laden with coal dust, and in later years there were explosions in the Crow's Nest mines resulting in many fatalities. The worst disaster in Canadian mining history occurred in the nearby Hillside Mine in 1914 when 189 men lost their lives.

After his two days underground, Guy worked in the office for the rest of the week, mapping the underground "streets" on the plan of the mine on which the monthly progress was recorded. There, he also tested samples of coal and coke, and wrote reports for the head office of the British Columbia United Gold Fields whose owners were in France. They had bought the company after the Frank Slide had buried the spur line to the mine.

Just two years before Guy arrived in Frank, early on the morning of April 29, 1903, ninety million tons of rock had swept down from Turtle Mountain on the sleeping town of 600 people, burying seventy of them in their beds. He was interested in the geology of the rock slide as well as the vivid stories the survivors had to tell of that fateful night. He was particularly impressed by the station agent, Sid Choquette, on duty at the time of the rock slide and expecting the "Spokane Flyer," already overdue from the west. When the station agent heard a rumble and roar, which others dismissed as the sound of the train crossing the trestle bridge, he set out to investigate and found the track buried under tons of rock while more continued to rain down. Choquette considered the railway his sacred trust. He grabbed his lantern, and with clouds of dust dimming the light, he clambered over masses of rock to reach the clear track just in time to stop the oncoming train.[17]

After growing up in staid, small-city Ottawa and years of intense study for his engineering degree, Guy experienced the kind of freedom that only occurs early in life. He had a cayuse, the hardy, sure-footed Indian breed of pony available at the livery stable belonging to the mine, and would ride into the nearby towns of Frank or Blairmore where there were young people. Often on weekends they arranged to make trips on mountain trails or sometimes head thirty miles east as far as Pincher Creek where the foothills approached the open prairie. If they went westward, through the gap above Frank they could see the Oldman River flowing through wide flat rangeland enclosed by mountains, with the outstanding conical peak of Crow's Nest Mountain standing alone. If they followed the South Kootenay Pass trail, they reached a summit from which they could see the Flathead Plains of Montana. Riding by himself up Gold Creek past the mine, Guy could follow a trail that led through valleys among the razorbacks of the Livingstone Range.

During his year at Lille, a forest fire swept through from British Columbia, leaping across Gold Creek valley and threatening the town of Lille. Preparations were made to evacuate the women and children by train, while the men cut fire guards, set back fires, and safeguarded the dynamite cache. Despite these excitements, the novelty of the job had worn off by the end of his first year, and Guy was increasingly disenchanted with his life in Lille. He recalled the words of Oliver Hall, the engineer he had replaced. After giving Guy a tour of his new responsibilities, Hall explained why he was leaving, "A mining engineer in a coal mine has little opportunity to improve his position, the place to go is back East and get into hard-rock mining." The only advancement Guy could expect from the Lille coal mine was to become an executive permanently seated behind a desk in an office, and already he knew that was the part of the job he liked least.[18]

In a chance meeting with a surveyor passing through from Edmonton, Guy caught the excitement of the land boom taking place in the North and heard about the need for engineers to work as surveyors. He had heard the call to explore and map the great unknown areas of the northern wilderness and in his imagination a new path was opening before his eyes. But first he had to get there and find a job.

The transcontinental railway passed through Crow's Nest Pass on its way to Calgary, an important railway centre in the midst of a real estate boom, as homesteaders flooded into the west. In Calgary, Guy boarded the train to Edmonton, recently named the capital of the new province, and as he rode north he watched the landscape change from ranchland to northern prairie. The line ended at Strathcona, on the south side of the North Saskatchewan River. There he got into a horse-drawn bus that rattled down the steep river bank to a low-level bridge and carried him up to the city of Edmonton. Guy found a modest white clapboard hotel, Riverside House, noted for its moderate rates and good meals, with stabling for horses.

He set out at once to find work and spotted the sign, "Driscoll and Knight, Land Surveyors," with a smaller notice underneath, "No Englishman need apply." This referred to upper-class Englishmen, known as "remittance men," who were not fitted for practical work. Knowing he was acceptable on that score, Guy entered the office and met Alfred Driscoll. Driscoll then sent Guy off to find a government survey party in need of an assistant, somewhere on the prairies. Was his mission real, or was Driscoll testing him to see if he had the necessary perseverance and stamina to be a surveyor? If Driscoll was testing him, Guy had passed with flying colours and had now embarked on his life's work.

TWO — THE SURVEYOR: 1906–1919

When Guy Blanchet arrived in Edmonton in 1906 with the ambition to become a surveyor, the tidal wave of land-hungry immigrants from all corners of Europe and the United States was in full swing. That same year also saw the completion of the Canadian Northern Railway as far as Edmonton, bringing 300 to 500 immigrants each day, the majority of them farmers hoping to take advantage of the government's offer of free land. Under the Dominion Lands Act enacted in 1872, each settler was granted a quarter section of free land, providing he lived on it and cultivated it for three years.[1] Most of the readily arable land had been mapped into townships, each of the thirty-six sections measuring one square mile, and all numbered in such a way that every property could be identified on a master chart. Much of the land south of a line between Edmonton and Prince Albert had been surveyed, but the huge area to the north was still relatively untouched.

There was no shortage of work for surveyors around the city of Edmonton, as a wave of optimism led to skyrocketing inflation in land values, and farmers on the edge of the city sought to make their fortunes by subdividing their land into town lots. Alfred Driscoll gave Guy his first job as an assistant to the surveyor who was creating housing plots in the Pembina area on the western edge of Edmonton. While this was not challenging work it was a good review of the techniques that Guy had learned during his engineering course at McGill, such as using a transit with a rod to measure angles of elevation, a Gunter's chain[2] or a metal tape to measure distance, the importance of levelling the ground being measured, and the spherical trigonometry needed to make the calculations.[3]

Having demonstrated some competence after a few months on the job, Guy was recalled to the office and asked to take charge of a survey of timber limits on the North Saskatchewan River in eastern Saskatchewan. This, being strictly a measurement of the area to which the government had sold the rights to cut timber, did not require a high degree of accuracy and could be done using only a compass and chain. The client, Mr. Finger, an important man in the lumber industry at The Pas, met Guy in Prince Albert and they travelled together by sleigh to Fort à la Corne, a Hudson's Bay Company post near the old French fort. Having hired the survey party that was waiting at Fort à la Corne and arranged the transportation, he then left Guy to take charge.

It was the middle of December when Guy and the hired party set off on a six-day journey by horse-drawn toboggans, each eighteen feet long, two feet wide, and capable of carrying a thousand pounds. They followed the dog trail, the mail-route trail made by men on snowshoes with their dog teams, through the light woodlands of muskeg country. They carried only the bare necessities: a toboggan load of fresh meat, no cook, no utensils and no tents. While each man would naturally have carried a knife, cups and fingers were all they had to eat with, and they called it "the soup trail." Six days later when they reached the small settlement of Red Earth, on the Carrot River, they picked up their camping equipment, the bulk of their supplies and their cook, all having been brought upriver from The Pas. The timber cruiser, who would assess and record the marketable timber, joined the party there as well, and he taught Guy much about woodlands and winter life in the woods.

On this survey, Guy had a variety of learning experiences. Around Christmas, the temperature dropped to sixty degrees below zero and hovered there for weeks, and the air was filled with tiny frost particles. The men from the area were dressed for the cold. They had good tents and stoves, and Guy had a woven rabbit-skin robe for sleeping. Despite the low temperatures, the party sometimes encountered thin ice covering air holes, where a man falling through would have his clothing instantly frozen into a suit of armour on contact with the air. The timber stands were on the banks of the meandering, swampy Sipanic River, which sometimes flooded long stretches of ice and caused moccasins to freeze, making for painful walking over long distances.

By March the temperature had moderated and Guy had his first taste of snow blindness from the brilliant sun reflecting from the frozen surface of the snow. It felt like having cinders in his eyes, and he could hardly keep them open, but it was still painful even when they were shut. The only treatment available in the bush was to put wet tea leaves on the eyes at night, and blacken the skin around them in the daytime.

More inconvenient was the arrival of a North West Mounted Police[4] officer early in the survey to arrest the cook for a previous breach of the law. He had been a good cook, and a member of the crew volunteered to take his place, saying that he had worked as a cook on the railways. This man had been the worst complainer about the meals, had no imagination when it came to cooking, and had a mean streak as well, hating to see hungry men scoffing down the products of his efforts.

When the work was finished, the survey party set out to return to Prince Albert by the winter-mail dog trail from Cumberland House. The trail was firm, having been packed down by loaded sleighs and snowshoes after successive snowstorms, but it was also narrow with deep soft snow on either side. The lead horse could not stay on the trail but continually plunged off into the deep snow, having to be extricated with great effort. They tried one horse after another without success, until as a last resort they put the laziest horse in front and he slowly and carefully picked his way along the hard centre of the trail with the others following meekly behind.

Back in Edmonton, Guy was asked to make another timber limit survey far to the west in the foothills of the Rockies in the summer of 1907. The area was on the Brazeau River, parallel to and north of the North Saskatchewan River. Their party consisted of five men and six horses. The job of packer for a pack train requires a special skill, but in this case the man hired was capable but short-tempered. After only three days out from their base, he objected to Blanchet's order

Surveyor's base-line cut — "like a door opening into the forest."

Courtesy of BC Archives, #1-68461

of travel and quit on the spot. Guy had been watching his method of working, took on the job himself, and the crew was able to carry on without the departed packer. As they continued up the trail through the great forests of the foothills, they came to large burned-over areas where windfalls continually blocked their path. When these were too high for the horses to jump, the party would have to stop and cut a clear path. Each such obstacle created unexpected delays. Guy had provisioned on the basis that it was to be a quick trip, with the result that on their return journey they were reduced to eating wild berries washed down with water for three days. Fortunately, they met another survey party, this one surveying a railway route. The group gave them food, and the chief, noticing that Guy's footwear was worn out, presented him with a pair of dancing shoes from his kit bag, neither a good fit nor suitable for the job.

One more timber survey in 1907 took Guy northwest of Edmonton to the vicinity of the old Fort Assiniboine on the Athabasca River. To reach it they were able to take their horses and wagon on the remains of a road cut a few years earlier by parties attempting to reach the Klondike. They carried a skiff for use on the river. The Klondikers were long gone, but Guy encountered two people left behind by the tide of humanity that had flowed north. One was an African-American from the deep south who was sitting in his cabin with his feet in the warm ashes of the large earthen fireplace. The other man, living near the ruins of Fort Assiniboine, had stopped there on the way to the Yukon and watched others heading north into the Swan Hills from which they never returned.

In his personal photograph album, Blanchet wrote, "Survey work was hard then, but interesting. One thing I remember is that I had a pair of Strathcona boots that had stripped the skin off my heels…every morning I had to take the over-night scab off… presently it was not too bad. Our evening walk home was from four to eight miles…We Were Men In Those Days."[5]

For three years Guy, based in Edmonton, worked at any survey jobs available. In that time two things became clear to him: he needed proper qualifications to make a living in this work; and the jobs that interested him most were those in challenging conditions in unmapped territory. The Dominion Land Survey was now working in the relatively empty northern two-thirds of the prairie provinces, and Guy returned to Ottawa briefly to take the qualifying examination to become an assistant to a Dominion Land Surveyor. After a year of articling under a commissioned surveyor he could take the final examination, and provided he passed, he would then become entitled to put the initials, D.L.S., after his name and be in charge of a survey party.

Some surveying had been done throughout the country since the eighteenth century with surveyors like David Thompson working for the Hudson's Bay Company and then the North West Company. The Geological Survey of Canada,[6] in existence since 1845, sent

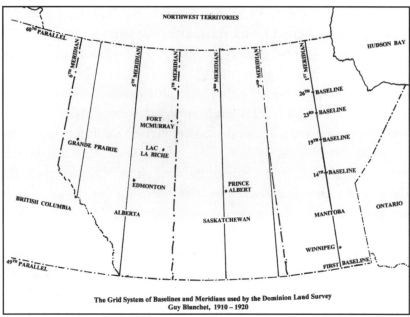

Map 1. Meridians and base lines of the western provinces of Canada, map by Gwyneth Hoyle.

its members off in all directions, using the rivers as their highways, hammers in hand to tap the rocks and find the telltale signs of minerals lurking below the surface of the land. They were followed by topographical surveyors with the task of mapping the land and all its features. The Dominion Land Survey came into existence in 1869 to fulfil an entirely different mandate.[7] Its responsibility was twofold: the careful, accurate measurement of the grid on which all maps of the country would be overlaid; and the subdivision of that grid into acreages suitable for the expected influx of settlers. The field of operation for beginning the work was the newly acquired area between the Red River Settlement and the Rocky Mountains, the broad, treeless plains of the prairies, just waiting for the first ploughs to turn them into fields of grain.

The huge checkerboard grid on which the country is mapped consists of meridians, 160 miles apart, running true north from the 49th parallel, theoretically to the North Pole. Every twenty-four miles along the meridians, there is a post marking the corner of a township, and the lines that join these markers are the base lines.

Because these must be located accurately, their survey was always done by fully qualified Dominion Land Surveyors.

As the buffalo disappeared from the plains, their place seemed to be taken by an army of surveyors, each one leading a group of about twenty men. The peak of this activity was reached in 1883, when there were 119 survey parties working in the southern third of the prairies, and by the end of that particular year over sixty million acres had been surveyed, divided into townships and quarter-section farm units. The most skilled of the surveyors were employed marking out meridian lines, running north and south, and base lines, east to west, to form an accurate grid of the whole western area. The extent of the Dominion Land Survey was mind-boggling, and the speed and accuracy with which it was accomplished is unique in the annals of surveying throughout the world.

Back from his first successful exam in 1909, Guy was appointed assistant to George Macmillan who was to survey base lines in the Peace River country. The area known as the Peace River District was the aboriginal homeland of several different Native tribes, but particularly the Beaver in the western part. As the fur traders penetrated the country, the Cree, from the woodlands to the east, sought to be the middlemen between the western tribes and the traders, and they had the benefit of arms. The result was constant tribal warfare. Peace River gets its name from the moment before 1760 when the tribes gathered at a point of land on the south side of the river, thereafter called Peace Point, and declared a truce. In addition to the fur trade, gold seekers had passed through and some had stayed, and Métis, trying to get beyond the boundaries of agricultural settlement, had moved into the area as well. Already this district was being touted by these few pioneers as the next great bonanza for settlers looking for free land.

As assistant on the survey, Guy's first task was to order the supplies for the crew of twenty men for the eight-month duration of the survey. The amounts were based on a daily ration for each man. He was shocked by the quantities involved — nearly two tons of flour and beef and about half a ton each of bacon and sugar. It was harder to gauge the essentials such as yeast and condiments, and the small luxuries that give variety to the diet, but all had to be bought in advance and any mistakes would show up months later, far from the source of supply.

As always on these northern base-line surveys, the first problem to solve was that of reaching the assigned area. While the base lines to be surveyed were south of Grande Prairie and stretching west to the British Columbia border, the only way to get there was by following the traditional trails established by the aboriginal people, a route that would take them many miles north of where they were trying to go. The crew set out in sleighs on the winter road to Athabasca Landing in March of 1909, followed by a pack train of freighters carrying their supplies. This route was in regular use and every twenty miles were stopping places with hay for the horses and shelter where the men could cook a meal and bed down on the floor. The trail continued west and north, across the still-frozen Lesser Slave Lake, crossed to the north bank of the Peace River, and arrived at the old fur-trade post of Fort Dunvegan, where Alexander Mackenzie had passed through on his epic journey west.[8]

Fort Dunvegan, soon to be abandoned, was in such a state of decline that it could not supply any oats or hay for the horses, and the man in charge advised travelling about twenty miles southwest to Spirit River where a rancher could supply feed for the horses. The date was May 3, and the breakup of the Peace River could come at any time. The river valley they had to cross below Dunvegan is very deep, with steep enclosing walls. They had to lower the wagons down with ropes, then found the ice so dangerous that they hauled the wagons across the river by hand and then led the horses over one at a time. They climbed out of the valley, set up camp high on the south bank of the river. During the night they were wakened by a rumble that grew to a roar. By morning the whole river was in motion, and they watched the spectacle of the ice going out.

The party pushed on to Spirit River and waited there for the prairie grass to grow sufficiently to restore the horses to strength. It was the end of May before they reached the Smoky River near where the work was to begin. They had been on the trail for three months, and they would be working from the 6th meridian west to the British Columbia boundary.

Courtesy of Richard Blanchet

A group of surveyors loaded and ready for the portage in the railway belt of British Columbia, 1910. Guy Blanchet, second from the right.

On this first experience with a Dominion Land Survey, Guy not only absorbed the features of the landscape, but learned the routine of a survey camp. The main responsibility of the chief was to run a properly located line, sometimes based on astronomy. He also made notes on the soil and the terrain, as well as being in charge of the whole group. Each morning, one axeman set out first to break trail through the bush, continually glancing back to make sure he was still on line. Behind him came the remaining axemen, chopping on alternate sides of the line. The picket man walked immediately behind the last axeman and put up pickets lined in by one transit man. Setting up his instrument, sighting on Polaris, checking his back sight by a picket man behind, the transit man flipped his telescope to sight another few hundred yards forward to a convenient new sighting. The chainmen and levellers, usually about one-half-day's cut behind the axemen, worked along the line in two-man teams, making the ground level enough for accurate measurement with the Gunter's chain or metal tape. Near the end of the previous day's cut was the base-line transit man, who was either observing, or helping the mounders. The mounders were usually two miles behind the axemen and their job was to build permanent monuments to mark the survey. In this way, the front transit man "dragged his survey forward, chain by chain, creek by creek, and year by year."[9]

As assistant to the chief, Guy was the forward transit man and often having to spend long hours at a station, he asked the picket man to choose if possible a location with some pleasant feature. "Once when I was stationed on a high hill overlooking a valley, I heard a strange sound far below me. It was not an animal. There were two notes. I focused my transit on the valley and searched for it. I saw a teepee with smoke curling from it and nearby a WOMAN and a CHILD. [Blanchet's capitals]. They seemed so out of place in this wild empty country. These voices stirred memories. Then came the call from the picket man for a new station. I moved on and never saw them again."

The chief hired a Cree guide, Celestin Gladu, who knew the country of the Smoky River, and he would locate and open up the trail from one camp to the next. Guy enjoyed travelling with Celestin, "I learned some Cree and of more importance, Indian ways. I received what I considered a compliment from him as reported by one of the men, 'Good work, good walk, not much talk.' Celestin had preserved a trait of the Indians of the old days on the trail — a gesture could save many words, but at the camping place he was a good talker." He also preferred fresh meat to the heavily cured pork that was standard survey fare, and when he became meat hungry and had the opportunity, he went hunting and supplied the camp.

The Smoky River rises near Mount Robson and flows with a turbulent course through the foothills and across the plateau until it reaches the Peace River. When the survey line reached the river, they had to swim the horses across and build a raft to ferry the men and supplies—the whole process leading to a few mishaps. On one occasion, the cook, carrying his sourdough in a bucket, was plunged into the river but managed to gain footing and hold the sourdough over his head until he was rescued.

As transit man, Guy had to carry the delicate instrument in its heavy protective case, and sometimes looked for a shorter, easier path to follow. On one occasion, trying to avoid fording a couple of

Courtesy of Richard Blanchet

The first survey group to be Guy Blanchet's charge, 1911. "I was 27... in some ways old and in others a bit young for the job." Blanchet is in the back row, fourth from the right. His favourite cook, Bill Behan, is in the centre of the back row.

streams and extra climbing, he set off following the crest of a valley ridge, holding to the talus slope, which was clear of fallen trees, another awkward hazard. All was going well until he came to a "V" cut made by a spring freshet. While balancing the transit on his shoulder, he had to make two steps at the bottom of the "V" over loose sand and gravel. His first cautious step immediately started debris pouring over the cliff, threatening to carry him along. He froze on the spot, unable to move. When he could trust his legs and made the leap to safety, he saw the stream of material he had unleashed pouring in a flood down to the valley, a thousand feet below. He resolved then and there to take no more chances with shortcuts.

Guy had permission to leave the survey early in December and return to Ottawa by train to prepare for his final examinations, which in addition to mathematics, astronomy and survey techniques, involved the legal aspects of the profession. He passed successfully, and now fully qualified he received his first assignment to survey the 23rd base line between the 4th and 5th meridians, passing just north of Fort McMurray.

Guy set about planning the logistics of the journey to the area to be surveyed and assembling a typical twenty-man crew. Of these twenty men, the most essential after the chief, were the packer, in charge of moving the camp as the line advanced, and the cook, on whose shoulders rested the contentment of the group. He hired a packer he knew from the Peace River expedition and advertised for a cook. The man who applied "was short and stocky, bald and toothless, and had the map of Ireland on his face and its brogue accentuated by a recent visit to a pub. He appealed to me and I engaged him. This was old Bill." He was not only a good cook, but his loyalty and Irish wit kept morale high in bad times. Bill Behan turned out to be such a good choice that Guy rehired him each season for most of the next ten years, and named a lake for him in northern Alberta.

It took ingenuity, a knowledge of routes and transportation systems, and the co-operation of the Hudson's Bay Company to reach the assigned area. In 1911, Guy and most of his crew travelled on their own scow in company with the Athabasca Brigade, the HBC's fleet of twenty-five scows making the annual trip from Athabasca Landing to Fort McMurray, the route used to supply the fur-trade posts on the Mackenzie River. This historic fur-trade route had been in use since 1885 and would continue to be used until the rail line to Fort McMurray made it obsolete.

Everyone heading north converged on the little community of Athabasca Landing at the beginning of May, and the place hummed with activity in the season before the ice went out. The sawmills were busy converting logs into planks for the shipyard to build scows to a standard pattern. In 1911 the chief of the HBC brigade was Captain Ernest Haight, who had not only spent many years with the Brigade, but had led a contingent of Canadian boatmen up the Nile in the relief of Khartoum in 1884.[10] The various groups heading north, including the Northern Traders (an established fur-trading company vying with the HBC) and the Anglican and Catholic Oblate missions, were in keen competition to secure the best guides and steersmen for their scows. That same year George Douglas, whom Guy would later come to know well, was travelling with the HBC Brigade on his way to Great Bear Lake and the Coppermine, but it would be years before they met.[11] Guy did meet

Scenes from the Athabasca Brigade. "At the Big Cascade a too-wide river dropped over the limestone ledge, a six-foot drop in low water, almost smooth except for the back wave in times of flood."

Inspector Denny LaNauze of the RNWMP (the forerunner of the RCMP), on his way north on police business. Their interests and paths would cross again over the years.

The loading of the scows began only after every scow was in the water long enough to soak the green lumber and tighten the seams, and when it was completed all moved off together in one grand exodus heading North. This was a time of relaxation until they reached Grand Rapids, where it was necessary to portage using

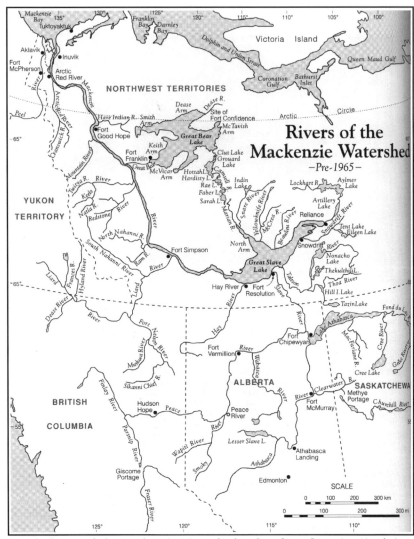

Map 2. *Rivers of the Mackenzie Watershed, taken from* Canoeing North into the Unknown, *114.*

a wooden railway built on an island in the centre of the channel. Then followed eighty miles of turbulent water that climaxed in the Big Cascade, a six-foot drop where scows were sometimes hung up and in danger of breaking, just a few miles before they reached Fort McMurray where the Clearwater River enters from the east.

At Fort McMurray, those heading north transferred to an HBC paddlewheel steamer. Blanchet and his party unloaded, stored part of their tons of supplies for later use when the base line reached McMurray, and began tracking their scow up the Clearwater River for sixty miles of swift water to the beginning of the survey. A pack train of horses, travelling light up the dog trail from Lac la Biche, met them at the beginning of the survey on the 4th meridian, the boundary between Alberta and Saskatchewan. More supplies were transferred to the farther end of the line by the HBC using water transportation up the Wabasca River. All the planning for these complicated logistics had to be done well in advance.

By early summer they had reached the marker left by the crew that had surveyed the 4th meridian, marking the beginning of the job. They now had to cut a straight six-foot wide swath through the boreal forest, clearing it for a winter sleigh road, for one hundred and fifty miles until they reached the mark left on the 5th meridian, building a mound every sixty miles to mark each range. Additionally, the ground for several miles on either side of the line was explored and the information included in the final report for the maps, which would be completed by the staff in Ottawa. In early February there was a great sense of anticipation as they approached the closing point, which would reveal the accuracy of the survey. Guy stood at the marker post of the 5th meridian listening to the ring of the axes, watching the trees falling, the transit man keeping his line true on its course. When the picket man took his point from the transit, it was a mere three feet south of the post — a remarkable achievement to have covered that distance so accurately in a straight line that allowed for the curvature of the earth's surface.[12]

On the first survey on which he was "Chief," Guy devised a portable table for the cook tent where the men could sit for their breakfast and dinner, making life easier for the cook and pleasanter for the men. It consisted of a cribwork affair, measured in axe-lengths and quickly knocked together at each camping site, which supported a strip of canvas with laths tacked on at close intervals and covered with oilcloth. At each camp the men quickly put together tree-trunk benches supported by blocks, and across these blocks they placed stringers or supports on which the table could be rolled out.

During this survey the mail packet reached them in November and contained instructions for Guy to complete the 23rd base line, and then go south to finish the 19th base line, abandoned by a previous crew that had bogged down in muskeg. On receiving these instructions, he left his assistant in charge and went south to Edmonton to arrange for new supplies. At that time of year the only method of travel was by dog team. Guy made his way to Fort McMurray where, finding that most of the men were out on their traplines and the trader could not spare his dogs, he arranged with the poorest man in the settlement to take him to Lac la Biche with his dog team. They had only made a day's travel when the man began making excuses to return home. Guy bought the dogs from him and continued on his way, learning to manage the team as he went.

At first he found the "dog trot" faster than a walk but slower than running. It was hard on his leg muscles, which were almost too stiff to move in the mornings, but gradually he adjusted. At a Native camp along the way he picked up a companion, John MacDonald, who was a guide on the Athabasca Brigade. MacDonald taught Guy all the tricks for managing a dog team, and they camped each night with MacDonald's friends along the trail, as far as Lac la Biche. There, Guy hired a horse and cariole and let the dogs loose. After reaching Athabasca Landing he completed the trip to Edmonton in the first automobile he had ever seen, a dilapidated Model T Ford, making the run in six hours instead of the usual two days.

It was well into December before Guy had completed the arrangements for the next job and started back to the survey. After the luxury of an automobile drive to Athabasca Landing, he hired a Métis with his dog team to take him up the Athabasca River. Christmas was approaching as they reached Grand Rapids on the river, and the end of the good trail. After a mild snowy night, without a tent, his guide suddenly announced the need to return to the Mission to make his annual confession. Guy soon realized that arguments were useless as it was the celebration of New Year that was attracting his guide back to the Landing. The guide turned south and left Guy to continue north on foot through the ice jams on the river and up the deep river valley where he spotted the survey

Courtesy of Richard Blanchet

Courtesy of Richard Blanchet

Horses played an important role in the early surveys.

line and followed it to rejoin his crew. During the nine months of this survey, in addition to making a closure of the line, Guy had travelled by every available means and, best of all, the experience had satisfied his inner needs for variety and challenge.

In Edmonton he hired Robert Logan to be second assistant, taking the place of A.N. Narraway who was returning to Ottawa.

Logan would later write of his experiences on completing the survey of the 19th base line that had been abandoned years earlier because of difficulties with the muskeg, and because the party became snowed in and nearly starved. "The Chief [Blanchet] not only had to keep careful check on the accuracy of his assistants with the transit, level, and chain, but had to direct and check on the work of all sub-parties; doctor horses, dogs, and men, when necessary; plan for supplies and mail, and strive to keep everybody in good humour and pulling together." Logan also had a story about the naming of Fawcett Lake: "Sid Fawcett, [Blanchet's first assistant] always carried a big 45 revolver, hoping to shoot a bear. One evening, coming to camp along the pack-trail at the edge of a creek, Sid and a big bear almost bumped noses, neither having any thought of anything except where he was putting down his feet. The bear stood up, snorted, and almost rolled over backward as he jumped off the trail into the middle of the stream. Sid was so surprised the he was almost in camp before he remembered the big revolver hanging from his belt. The bear has been forgotten but Sid's name was placed on the map…a few miles north of where the 5th meridian crosses the Athabasca River."[13]

The ground was solidly frozen in March when Blanchet and his crew reached the point at which the previous surveyor had given up, and Guy knew they had two months before the thaw set in, by which time they would be on solid ground. The survey completed, Guy returned home to Ottawa in September for a holiday while he awaited his next assignment. He had been in the northern wilds for eighteen months.

From 1911 until the end of 1919 Guy Blanchet was in charge of base-line surveys in the north of Alberta and Saskatchewan, with the exception of 1915 when he was east of Lake Winnipeg around the area of the Berens River. In his own words, "Technically, all base lines are much the same…a party of twenty-one men and thirty-one horses…a sky line creeping across the country ignoring obstacles, leaving a trail of monuments behind to mark its passage even after the forest closes in and the elements partly obliterate them. The humans engaged on the survey are anonymous after enlivening the line as they passed along it with the ringing of axes and crashing of trees, and with the community life of the camps where they paused." The weather, the nature of the country and incidents beyond the routine of daily life were all that distinguished one base-line survey from another.

In his descriptions of surveys, while he names nearly every Native or Métis person he meets, the members of the crews are anonymous, with the exception of Bill Behan — "Old Bill" — the cook. It was customary to employ Native guides to locate the trails that passed through their lands, and many of his stories are based on his relationship with them. On a later trip when he needed to raft down the McKay River to investigate an area, Guy chose Albert Tait, an educated Métis and a fine man, but unfortunately a garrulous one. Albert was arthritic and a poor walker, so on their long walk back Guy regularly outpaced him to stay out of earshot. By travelling late, they could reach the survey camp, but Albert asked permission to stop and rest and come in the next day. When he had not arrived by noon, Guy went back and found him just where he had left him, a note thoughtfully pinned to his coat stating that he had stopped because he was tired and the illness came on after Guy had left him at his own request. Albert was alive but weak, and was given a horse to ride until he recovered.

During the wild passage down the McKay River, Guy and Albert met a Native hunter travelling upstream in a birchbark hunting canoe. He had recently left "civilization" — Fort McKay — and after some talk in Cree, Albert announced, "This fellow says that there is a great war among the white men. He does not know who or where." Blanchet said, "Maybe moccasin telegram." "No" said Albert, "this man says war big, big and far, far." When the mail reached the camp late in August 1914, with an out-of-date newspaper, they finally understood the cataclysmic events in Europe.

On that particular survey, Guy had worked with the "bull gang" most of the time, clearing trees for the line, and they reached the upland area of the Birch Mountains to complete the survey late in November. When they arrived at the closing post, Guy complimented the men on the fine job they had done, and the picket man replied, "We had to work like fools to keep up with you, and now we have worked ourselves out of a job with winter coming on." Guy did not

Courtesy of BC Archives, #1-68465

Eileen Taylor Blanchet, who married Guy in 1914, on a boat on Lake Winnipeg in 1915, accompanying her husband on his way to survey the area around the Berens River, following their holiday at the Lake of the Woods.

explain that he had an appointment to keep in Ottawa a few days later. He was getting married to Eileen Gardner Taylor, and he was looking forward to a good long break in their own home before he headed out on his next assignment.

The wedding took place in Ottawa on December 12, 1914, with Guy's older brother, Sidney, a doctor from Saranac Lake, New York, as one of the witnesses. Eileen, four years younger than Guy, was born in Saint John, New Brunswick, where her father had been a bank manager. Eileen's mother had died in 1902 when Eileen and her two sisters were in their teens, but she had been buried in Ottawa where she was born, and where two of her brothers, both doctors, still lived.[14]

Guy had met Eileen Taylor in Ottawa in 1913 while he was home for several months between survey trips, and just before he left for the area north of Fort McMurray for the survey just completed. After a whirlwind courtship, they had become engaged. Perhaps this had given Eileen an inkling of the life that lay ahead. She would need to be self-sufficient and resourceful, being married to a man who thrived on challenge and adventure, and who was in love not only with her, but with the northern landscape.

Courtesy of Janet Blanchet

Florence Blanchet, Eileen Taylor and Guy Blanchet, in Ottawa about 1913.

The first time Guy was put in charge of a survey, he asked an official in the departmental office in Ottawa for information about the area to which he had been assigned. He was told, "Never ask the office for information. You are supposed to know your job or you wouldn't have been given it. Here, we know nothing of the country or how the survey should be carried on." All that head office wished to hear from a surveyor when the job was completed, were the words, "Survey completed, closing satisfactory." Since all appointments were for the duration of the assignment, a surveyor knew that his work was satisfactory only when he was given a new job to do. At the same time, the department would accept no excuse for a job not completed, and would look for a better man to finish the job. Understanding this, when he ran into an impassable muskeg on his next base-line survey, Guy completed all that was possible, took his crew out to Edmonton for a few weeks until freeze up, and went back just before Christmas to find their line and finish the job.

The word "impossible" was unacceptable both to the office in Ottawa, and to Blanchet. When travelling with their horses on the construction train from Edmonton to Fort McMurray, they were stopped just in time to watch the bridge over the Christina River being washed out by the spring flood. They could carry on from there with the pack train of horses, but to get men and supplies to their starting point would require several trips over muskeg just beginning to thaw. After the second trip, the packer announced it would be impossible to get the remaining supplies. The supplies had been carefully calculated for the season and were essential, so Guy decided he would go back himself with the assistant packer. On the way, they were lucky to meet local Natives who knew a route around the worst of the wet areas, and in two days of hard riding they were back with all the supplies. In addition to refusing to accept that anything was impossible, Guy also strongly believed in the principle that the leader should not ask a man to do what he is not willing to do himself.

Living in close quarters with the crew for months at a time, the head of a survey team was always addressed as "Chief" rather than by his first name. This protocol preserved his authority by keeping a certain reserve, allowing easy association but not familiarity with the rest of the men. He was responsible not only for completing the job properly, but also for their well being and safety, and maintaining a harmonious camp. Only once on all of his northern surveys did Guy have occasion to fire one of his men. He had chosen to make a winter survey with part of the crew to avoid the muskeg, and had arranged with the packer to rendezvous with the bulk of the supplies on May 1 at a designated point. Food was beginning to run short as they approached the meeting place, and Guy, with one of the crew, went ahead in search of the pack train. Twenty-five miles north he found a cache with signs that the packer had gone back for another load. The two men took what they could carry and returned to camp, finding the cook scraping the bottom of his pot. Two days later the pack train strolled into camp, the packer quite unconcerned and even riding on one of the horses — something that was absolutely taboo in the North. It was the only time in Guy's experience that a food cache had not been placed on time and, having a party of men dependent on it, he fired the packer on the spot.

The regulations stated firmly that women were not allowed on survey parties, but rules sometimes have to be broken. One year when his favourite cook was not available, Guy had hired a stranger who found he could not keep up with the job and quit somewhere in the country between the Clearwater River and the Methye Portage. Guy substituted for him with the cook's helper until they reached the Hudson's Bay post at Portage La Loche, where the factor suggested that he hire a Native girl. Alexandre, an old Native friend of Guy's, was willing to let his daughter, Marie, go along as cook as long as her husband could accompany her as cook's helper. Nothing was said about the nursing baby in the moss bag, who turned out to be the most contented person of all, "satisfied with survey rations as she received them, without embarrassment to herself, her mother or members of the crew," and never making a whimper.

On that particular survey, the terrain was such that the camp moved every day, very hard work for the horses in an area where there was no natural pasturage. As the oats were exhausted, they left the older horses near a pond where there was some old hay, to be picked up on their return: "One becomes attached to the horses and suffers with them, but the work must go on. After one move the packer arrived to tell me that Maggie, one of the small black horses was not able to make the trip back. I went with a small bag of oats to find her where he had left her, head down and trembling. While she nibbled at the oats, a bear crossed the line not far away, and Maggie did not even look up."

There might be thirty horses in a pack train, as individualistic as the men of the party. When a move had to be made with the pack train, the day started early, the packer and his helpers first having to find the horses by their bells. With the musical mingling of bells the horses arrived in camp. Even before breakfast, gear was packed, tents taken down and piled in a regular manner at the loading ground, with only the cook's tent still standing. The trail cutters would have located a camp some five miles ahead, as close as possible to the line. The laborious process of loading completed, the pack train moved off along the new trail, often with bad stretches of swamp, streams to cross and the windfall of old forest fires. When the new camping ground was reached, the horses were unloaded and turned loose. They might have a roll — one of the clumsiest actions of the horse — and then with a chorus of bells were led off to the best feeding grounds we could find, and if it did not satisfy they searched for themselves, perhaps remembering a good meadow back on the trail. I once had a Métis in charge of the horses who seldom had trouble finding them and asked him how he did it. He said, "If I was a horse what would I do? Then I go to where a horse would like to go...the horses are there."[15]

The final base-line survey that Blanchet made in northern Saskatchewan was in the Churchill River headwaters area, and it made a strong appeal to his sense of history and the days of the famous Churchill Brigade of the fur trade.[16] Always, before leaving Ottawa, Guy did a thorough search of the National Archives for material relating to the area. He found a letter from Alexander Mackenzie to his cousin Roderick instructing him to explore the Indian route to the Clearwater River in the hope of finding an easier

Courtesy of Richard Blanchet

Pierre Girard, whose mother was the prize in a shooting contest between the HBC and the North West Company at Fort Black.

route than the Methye Portage. With so much water in the area, horses were not used, but instead he had a crew of only five men with two canoes, and a small scow for the cook, which served as home base. On an island in one of the lakes, they came across a well-built house and store, occupied by a Scotsman and his wife. Guy asked if he would assist with the work, and was impressed with his reply, "No, laddie, me and the missus have lived here for twenty-five years without working and we have everything we need. Why should I work when I don't have to?"

In the course of this survey, Guy explored the remnants of an old abandoned fur-trade fort, Fort Black, guided to it by an eighty-year-old Indian, Pierre Girard, who claimed that his mother had been the prize in a shooting match held between the two competing companies, the North West and the Hudson's Bay, before 1821. The search for material on this fort, thought to have been built by Samuel Black,[17] engrossed Guy's spare hours for years to come.

The area of this last "southern" survey, was still so remote that it was travelled only by Native people. "Made Beaver," the coinage invented by the Hudson's Bay Company, was the currency at Portage La Loche and birchbark canoes were still being used as well as teepees. Guy could see the signs that this — to him — idyllic life was passing, and he was glad to be moving farther north to continue surveying areas that had been little touched by encroaching civilization. This is the paradox faced by all who love wilderness and write about their travels through it.

THREE — NORTH OF SIXTY: 1920–1923

By 1920 the northern surveys had gone beyond the areas of interest to potential settlers and, if further surveys were to be ordered, a new incentive would be needed. In August of that year the boost arrived in the form of an oil strike on the Mackenzie River, about fifty miles north of Fort Norman. News spread like wildfire throughout Canada and the United States, and it was expected that a stampede of prospectors would invade the area with the opening of the next navigation season. In anticipation of this, the Department of the Interior ordered a complete survey of the Mackenzie River and the shores of Great Slave Lake, to begin as early as possible in 1921.[1]

The river had been roughly mapped by Alexander Mackenzie in 1789, and John Franklin had carried out a track survey in 1824, which closely agreed with Mackenzie's chart, but the shorelines had never been surveyed. The Department now proposed to map the area in detail with the highest possible degree of accuracy. The survey was divided among three parties, each headed by a surveyor, and consisting of an engineer, a cook and eight men who would use two canoes, one on each side of the river to carry out traverses and instrument surveys. With such a small workforce, compared to the base-line surveys, every man was essential to the work. Each party was equipped with a scow to carry the supplies and to form the permanent base for the cook, as well as a motor boat to move the scow to the spot where the work ended each day.

The trio of scows was assembled at Peace River Crossing, and the survey parties enjoyed the voyage down the Peace River, with the challenge of running the chutes at Vermillion, and with the rapids on the Slave River before Fitzgerald (an Albertan community on the

Courtesy of Richard Blanchet

Jumping the Peace River chutes. The barge was loaded with canoes and supplies for the Mackenzie River survey, 1921.

river) adding interest. The first tractor to operate in the Northwest Territories hauled the scows across the portage to Fort Smith and a power schooner towed them westward across Great Slave Lake to the entrance to the Mackenzie River. The ice had gone out early that year, and fortunately the big lake was calm when they crossed it on June 7.

Guy Blanchet, in charge of one of the groups, began his survey at the tiny harbour on the south side, opposite Big Island where the Mackenzie splits into two channels. His survey proceeded smoothly at the rate of ten miles a day, north to Fort Simpson, the end of his section. The Liard River, rising in British Columbia, flows into the Mackenzie just before Fort Simpson and, after reaching the fort, Blanchet's party also surveyed twenty miles up the Liard, taking note of the power of the river in flood by the way the vegetation had been stripped from its banks to a height of twenty feet. The party then moved back to its starting point — which Blanchet called Wrigley Harbour — and continued surveying eastward along the south shore of Great Slave Lake.

While Guy had found the Mackenzie River impressive but uninteresting to travel, his romantic imagination was stirred by Great Slave Lake, with its long arms and channels, and its remote vastness, which seemed more typical of his vision of the North. As he was paddling a canoe into Hay River he saw his first airplane, a German Junker, one of two bought in New York in 1920 by Imperial Oil,[2] to service their property at Norman Wells. This was a harbinger of the future, and one that would play a large part later in his life. He and his party continued the survey along the south coast of Great Slave Lake to Fort Resolution, connecting with the benchmark of the previous survey of the Slave River. "No golden spike was used for our last monument — only an iron pipe with a bronze cap marked with a crown and the warning stamped on it: "Seven years' imprisonment for removal."

As the three crews caught the last steamer up the Athabasca River, heading for Fort McMurray and the railway, Guy expressed his regret at heading south: "For those who lived [in the North] or whose work brought them there, it was the unpleasant realization that once again their movements and activities were set by the clock and the calendar. In the case of northern surveys, for months Nature, the cook and the Chief had been in automatic control."

The steamer was crowded with 125 persons, including forty government employees, all leaving before the onset of winter, but their adventures were not yet over. The upstream journey was slow, river levels being lower than in the spring. Because of shoals and sandbars, the captain tied up to the bank eight miles short of Fort McMurray and announced that he could go no farther. It was a Friday, and the weekly train would be arriving at the terminus, thirty miles up the Clearwater River, and leaving for the south on the following day. Guy and another surveyor canoed into McMurray early on Saturday, wired the general manager of the railway in Edmonton to explain the situation, stressing the fact that there was a large government contingent on the steamer. The reply came back that the train would be held, but only until midnight on Saturday. Using all the survey canoes, fully loaded with their accumulated baggage, the men made several trips to get the whole group upstream to Fort McMurray where it was arranged to hire a power scow to take them up to the landing on the Clearwater. It was close to midnight as they struggled on foot up out of the steep river valley to the terminus, carrying all their baggage. They reached the station at 12:20 a.m. only to learn that the train had left on the dot of midnight.

A rough frame building passed as a hotel and the group bedded down there to wait — possibly a week — for the next train. An hour later, they were awakened by the smell of smoke and all managed to get out just before the ramshackle building was totally engulfed in flames. Fortunately, most of the luggage, and all of the survey notes from the summer were still at the station. A special train was sent from Edmonton two days later, and before they boarded it they took up a collection for the hotel proprietor.

Back at the office in Ottawa, as they were beginning the task of preparing the voluminous notes from nearly 2,500 miles of survey, including both shores of the Mackenzie River for a distance of one thousand miles, the surveyors were shocked to learn that the department had no plans to prepare maps from the information collected. Knowing that several northern transportation companies were keenly interested in having such maps, the surveyors took it upon themselves to write personally to the officials of each company suggesting that they contact the Minister of the Interior and stress how useful the maps would be for navigation and other purposes. This produced immediate results. The department reversed its decision, and the maps were given top priority.

The following year, 1922, the survey of Great Slave Lake was to be continued. This huge lake had first appeared on a map when Samuel Hearne sketched the outline, as described to him by his Native companions, for inclusion in the publication of his overland journey from Churchill to the mouth of the Coppermine River in 1771–72. He gave the lake roughly the correct shape but did not place it in its true position. Explorers, from John Franklin[3] to George Back[4] and the missionary-explorer Father Emil Petitot,[5] and others, all added details to the map, but none had surveyed it accurately and the existing maps were full of errors.

Guy was promoted to be in charge of three parties of surveyors who would work independently using the method they had used on the Mackenzie River survey. Because rivers, lakes and islands have irregular shapes, as opposed to base lines and meridians that follow straight lines for as far as the eye can see, they used a method called a "traverse," which measured the riverbanks, or the perimeters of lakes and islands in a series of straight lines between points. In the three groups on the Mackenzie River, the surveying had been done by two parties, each consisting of two men with a canoe using a transit and a rod, working on opposite sides of the river and advancing about ten miles a day. Precision depended on the transit man's ability, the length of the course, the light and whether the rod was held vertically. Certain conditions of sunlight, heat, haze and mirage made readings difficult. The measurements could be checked by a range finder for distance and the transit bearings used various checks as well as star sightings. To increase accuracy, a party from the Dominion Observatory would take observations at points 150 miles apart and set permanent concrete monuments, where the measurements could be checked and remeasured if necessary, making it a "controlled traverse." On Great Slave Lake the parties of surveyors would be working in groups of two along shorelines of islands and the mainland, and their measurements would be tied in to markers determined by astronomic observations.

Guy decided that the eastern arm, roughly a third of the area of the whole lake, and filled with islands, peninsulas and unknown channels, was the area in most urgent need of correction on the existing maps. This time each survey party was made up of only four men, and one of them would have to cook as well as paddle a canoe. Three other surveyors were appointed to head each party, Hugh Pearson was assigned to the south shore, Colin MacDonald, the north shore, and John Russell was given the task of surveying the islands. Each man ordered the supplies for his own party, which would be delivered as needed by the schooner, *Ptarmigan,* a two-masted vessel with a cabin, about thirty-five feet long. Guy co-ordinated and supervised the work from the ship, along with a pilot and an assistant.

For his pilot, Guy hired Souci Beaulieu, a Métis from the area near Fort Resolution, whose ancestors had a long tradition of guiding explorers.[6] The great-grandfather of Souci (diminutive for Joseph) had been a French-Canadian voyageur with the Churchill

Courtesy of Richard Blanchet

Guy Blanchet, cooking aboard the Ptarmigan, *with his pilot, Souci Beaulieu, 1923.*

Brigade who injured his back at Portage La Loche. On reaching Fort Chipewyan, he married a Chipewyan woman and remained in the area. His son, François, Souci's grandfather, was a canoe man with Alexander Mackenzie on his voyage to the Pacific Ocean in 1793, and in the 1820s he had set up the base at Fort Franklin on Great Bear Lake and kept it supplied with meat through the winter for John Franklin. With seven wives, François lived the life of a sultan, fathered a large family, was chief of the Yellowknife tribe, and was still hunting at the age of 85. One of his sons, Étienne — always known as King — was guide, in 1890, to Warburton Pike, the Englishman who travelled to the Barrens to shoot muskox and caribou. Pike, whose name is commemorated in Pike's Portage, the route from Great Slave Lake to Artillery Lake, immortalized King Beaulieu in his book, *The Barren Ground of Northern Canada,* alternately praising him as a brilliant guide and disparaging him as rapacious and ill-tempered.

Souci, the son of King, had inherited his father's grasping nature. He was a confident pilot in waters that he knew, but handed over the tiller to Guy in unfamiliar areas, complaining of his poor eyesight to avoid losing his reputation should they run aground.

Courtesy of Richard Blanchet

John Hornby, crossing Great Slave Lake, encountered Blanchet and his survey crew on the Ptarmigan, *1923.*

Guy, with his deep interest in northern history, spent hours on the quarterdeck with Souci, listening to his stories, while working out the intricate geography of the area.

In 1922, at the start of the survey as the *Ptarmigan* was making its way across a rough stretch of Great Slave Lake, towing a string of seven canoes behind it, they encountered a lone canoeist making his way across to Fort Resolution. This was John Hornby, the quixotic Englishman who had come to Canada in 1904. He had lived for several years around Great Bear Lake where he had known Vilhjalmur Stefansson and Dr. R.M. Anderson, who several years later would be leaders of the Canadian Arctic Expedition.[7] In 1911, when George Douglas and his associates built their cabin on Great Bear Lake, Hornby was living nearby with the priest, Father La Rouvière who, along with Father LeRoux, was later murdered by Inuit. Most recently Hornby had survived the previous two winters as a hermit in a state of semi-starvation in a hut near Fort Reliance on the north shore of Great Slave Lake.

Guy remembered meeting Hornby in his early days as a surveyor working out of Edmonton in 1906, and had certainly heard of his athletic feats, including his fifty-mile run beside a horse from Edmonton to Lac Ste. Anne and, more sensationally, the 100-mile run to Athabasca Landing in twenty-four hours. Hornby, who had been educated at one of England's finest public schools, spoke with a cultivated accent that belied his ragged appearance.[8]

The *Ptarmigan* was heading for the channel on the north shore of the eastern arm of the big lake that Blanchet, using the existing maps, believed to be the only passage by which they could reach their destination at the eastern end of the lake. Hornby described a more sheltered southern channel, the one by which he had just travelled in his canoe, and, with Souci Beaulieu's approval, undertook to guide them through it. They put Hugh Pearson off on the south shore, struck across toward the north shore where Colin MacDonald was to do his work, and left John Russell among the islands. It was sometime later as they were travelling in the north channel that Hornby remarked that MacDonald had been put off on an island — still quite far from the north shore — again contrary to the map that Blanchet was using. In the cabin of the *Ptarmigan*,

Courtesy of Richard Blanchet

The Ptarmigan, *used for transportation on Great Slave Lake.*

Hornby sat down and drew from memory a freehand map of the intricate configuration of islands, peninsulas and channels making up the eastern arm of Great Slave Lake, which he had learned from his solitary wanderings by canoe, and which proved to be remarkably accurate. After spending several days working together on the vessel, Guy invited Hornby to join him on the rest of the survey but Hornby declined, having decided instead to head south to Edmonton.

While the three surveyors worked in their assigned areas, Guy charted the channels through the islands, investigated the land formations and kept in touch with the three survey parties, delivering supplies as they needed them. It is one of the prerogatives of surveyors to suggest names for the various features. Guy named the channel that Hornby had shown them, Hornby Channel, and the wide channel along the north shore Hearne Channel for Samuel Hearne, the first white man to have seen it. Names can also arise from events as they occur. Hugh Pearson, surveying a bay which turned out to be deeper than expected, on a warm day while the cook, who had bread rising in the canoe, kept complaining, "My bread is going wild," named the bay "Wildbread Bay."

Where possible, Guy liked to preserve the traditional names and asked Souci for the name that the old people used for a prominent point that George Back had named Point Keith. Guy heard the name as "Pekanatui" after Souci had repeated it several times so Guy could write it down phonetically. When submitted to the Geographic Board, it was at first rejected until Guy insisted that it was historically correct. When he returned the following summer and told Souci they would camp at Pekanatui Point, Souci said, "I tole you Point à Tuer ...not Pekanatui" — it had been a caribou pass where the women would drive the caribou on to the point where the hunters would ambush and kill them. However, Pekanatui, the supposedly old Indian name preserved on the official map, was not a word in any language — and as Guy wrote in his unpublished memoir, "Apparently, I am the old Indian." In the detailed modern topographical map Pekanatui Point and Pointe à Tuer are adjacent to each other on Keith Island. The names of the surveyors can be seen in various other features.

Fort Reliance, at the easternmost end of Great Slave Lake where the Lockhart River enters the lake, had a good harbour. It had been the headquarters for George Back in 1833–35, at the time of his descent of the Great Fish River (later named the Back River). Only the chimneys and stone fireplaces remained of the original buildings, and a log cabin had been built around one fireplace in 1897 by Colonel C.J. "Buffalo" Jones, the American hunter collecting game for the Bronx Zoo. Guy visited these remnants and, accompanied by Souci, explored up the Lockhart River to the first cascade and continued on foot to visit the Tyrrell Falls, which plunge eighty-five feet into a deep canyon. To photograph the falls, Guy made his way over spray-swept ledges down into the canyon, while Souci kept his distance and warned him to take care, knowing that if anything happened to Blanchet it would reflect badly on the guide.

Before the summer was over, Guy and Souci climbed Pike's Portage, up through the chain of little lakes for twenty-five miles to Artillery Lake. Guy had his first glimpse of the Barrens, saw band after band of caribou swimming across the lake on their way south from the calving grounds. His imagination was stirred and he longed to go further, but the season was closing in. The three survey parties had finished their work and had to be collected before the *Ptarmigan* could set off across Great Slave Lake, towing its string of canoes, to catch the transportation south from Fort Smith.

The spirit of the North had infected Guy, and when spring arrived it seemed the most natural thing in the world to be heading down the Slave River again in 1923. Only the north arm of Great Slave Lake remained to be surveyed, and John Russell, who had been with Guy the previous summer, took his party to begin work in that area.

From what he had been told and from his own experiences, Guy realized the need for navigation aids on the big lake, and the Department of Marine in Ottawa had agreed to furnish a bell buoy and range lights if he would undertake the task of setting them up. Once again he could work from the *Ptarmigan*, and he hired Captain Mills, newly retired from service in the Hudson's Bay Company, to be engineer on the schooner, and one Native boy to help with the work. Captain Mills, having been in charge of the boat that travelled each summer from Fort Resolution down the Mackenzie River, was very familiar with navigation on the lake, and on the 1921 survey Guy named the first lake expansion on the Mackenzie River, Mills Lake, in his honour.

Three areas of the lake needed attention and those were the entrances to the three major rivers: the Slave, the Hay and the Mackenzie. Because of the continually shifting mud banks from the silt carried downstream, the entrance to the Slave River had to be approached from far out on the lake. Guy proposed to do two things: to mark where the river began by building a beacon on the last firm ground of the delta, high enough so that it could be seen above the willows growing there in profusion; and to anchor a bell buoy in the lake to mark the entrance to the river. The Department of Marine supplied the bell buoy, which turned out to be a huge 1,500 pound steel structure, six-feet high, topped by a heavy three-foot-wide bell.

First they built a substantial raft to carry this unwieldy structure, and then constructed heavy concrete anchors to hold it in position. Once it was completed they towed the whole contraption out to the correct location and waited to see how it would behave in the first storm. They did not have long to wait — spring is a stormy season on Great Slave Lake. Even with its thousand pound anchor, the buoy was swept away and went drifting aimlessly about the lake. It finally settled west of Fort Resolution, at the mouth of the Little Buffalo River, where the people complained bitterly that the bell was driving away the ducks.

They had more success at the entrance to the Hay River, setting lanterns on lobsticks as beacons, which the Anglican missionary promised to tend during the navigation season. Finally they built a beacon on the outermost island near the ship channel into the Mackenzie River, and finding the position of the reef that had previously damaged the steamer *Mackenzie River*, they placed a beacon opposite it on the south shore of the lake, and marked it on the map.

Having completed the navigation aids, the crew of the *Ptarmigan* proceeded carefully into the island-studded north arm of Great Slave Lake where Guy had arranged to meet John Russell and

Courtesy of Richard Blanchet

Courtesy of Richard Blanchet

Rock formations at the east end of Great Slave Lake.

to survey the settlement of Fort Rae. The community consisted of a group of small rocky islets where the Dogrib people had built cabins wherever they could find suitable ground. The Dogrib, a tribe of the Dene people, were a powerful group, reserved, independent and unsociable, and they became very upset seeing surveyors at work on their land, thinking that land was being taken away from them. After they chased Captain Mills who was holding the rod while Guy made observations through the transit, Guy called for a council with the priest, the Hudson's Bay factor and the local chief, Many Dried Geese, to explain that each family was entitled to 160 acres of land and this could all be arranged with the Indian Agent when he came to pay Treaty. This took place while Guy was in the settlement, and he experienced the night-long celebrations that included the drumming, the circle dance and games of chance, where some gambled away their treaty money, their clothes and, in one case, a wife.

Leaving John Russell to continue north into Marian Lake and the waterway leading to Great Bear Lake, Guy wanted to make a further exploration of the Barren Grounds that he had only glimpsed the year before, preparing to survey it the following year. He returned to Fort Resolution around the middle of August on the *Ptarmigan,* hoping to find two young Native men to go north with him, but was told by the HBC manager that the young men no longer knew the country and preferred to spend the summer loafing around the fort. As an alternative he discussed his plans with his old pilot, Souci Beaulieu, who despite his age — close to seventy — expressed a wish to see the Barren Grounds again and "fill his belly with the meat of caribou" before he died. Souci persuaded a reluctant Yellowknife, Black Basile, to join them, and the plan was settled.

As Guy was laying out what he considered the minimum supplies for a month, Souci objected, telling him that they were going into country where meat was plentiful and should live as the people did in the old days — sometimes feasting, sometimes in famine. The *Ptarmigan* took them to Fort Reliance, with one small canoe to begin their trip inland up Pike's Portage, and many years later Guy would write an article published in *The Beaver,* in the summer of 1960, about the trip, entitled "Exploring with Souci and Black Basile."

From the beginning Guy was fascinated by the relationship between the two men; Souci was the dominant figure. He always carried the lightest loads, frequently rested on his paddle, and told stories of his prowess as a hunter who could always find meat for his people. Black Basile, a descendant of the Yellowknife tribe who had never recovered from a crushing defeat from the Dogrib in the previous century, was the subservient one, who, in Souci's words, "can paddle because he has never had an engine and he is used to carrying loads." The two men talked together a great deal in Chipewyan, a language of which Guy knew little, and Souci was not helpful as an interpreter. "I told him to ask Basile if the country became flatter after we climbed the mountain. There was much talk and no answer. Finally I asked, 'What did Basile say?' Souci replied, 'Basile say nothing, just laugh.' He had said a great deal and had not laughed — he never did."

On reaching Artillery Lake they met the caribou, shot two of them and immediately the feasting began. They were still in sparsely wooded country with fuel for fire and stopped for a day to dry meat to carry with them. Once they were beyond the treeline, Guy learned how to cook using Arctic heather for fuel, or lacking that, found that black moss would provide enough heat if the pots were tightly lidded. While the two men had accepted the teachings of the Mission, being out in the ancestral lands had revived the old superstitions. Two dome-shaped hills on opposite sides of Artillery Lake were said to be the home of a giant beaver who owned the lake, and a huge muskrat, his slave. Guy was told to drop some tobacco into the lake to pay the beaver.[9] Souci, who by nature was never satisfied, said that the tribute had been very small and the beaver might be angry. Indeed, a squall blew up as they were making a wide traverse, threatening to swamp their canoe, and for once Souci threw his full weight into paddling.

They continued up the Lockhart River into Ptarmigan Lake and turned north into Clinton-Colden Lake (northeast of Great Slave Lake). Guy was aware of the earlier travels in that area by Samuel Hearne, George Back, Warburton Pike, and most recently by Ernest Thompson Seton, whose published accounts had all included sketch maps, none of them accurate.[10] Up to that point the way had been clear, but a look at a modern topographical map will show that Clinton-Colden was a sprawling body of water with a confusion of deep bays, headlands and islands. Souci Beaulieu had known this country only in winter hunting muskox, and he was depending on Basile, whose family group had hunted in this area when he was young. Basile climbed to the summit of a high island in Clinton-Colden Lake, studied the country and finally spotted the blue ridge that marks the Arctic divide at the Strait of Thanakoia. This was a well-known caribou crossing where the hunters could be sure of success. From a conical hill at the Strait of Thanakoia they viewed a large expanse of water, which Guy assumed was Aylmer Lake.

Guy longed to continue northward, exploring this alluring, empty country, but it was late in the season, the birds were returning south and wintry weather could begin any time. As they

Souci Beaulieu, with caribou kill, on the Barrens, 1923.

went north, Black Basile's greatest fear, inherited from his people, was of meeting Eskimo. This fear increased when he saw an ancient ring of tent stones and found a bit of fur which Guy identified as seal. Both Souci and Black Basile were anxious to return south, and in the homeward journey on familiar waters they travelled long hours making fast time. When Black Basile at last caught a glimpse of a clump of trees against the sky line, they doubled their efforts to reach them before camping to have the luxury of a real fire. As Souci crouched over it he said, "To me, a fire is like a father. I was glad to see the Barren Grounds again and the caribou. Strong meat brought back my young days, but never again will I leave the trees."

The *Ptarmigan* was waiting at Fort Reliance to take them across the lake to Fort Resolution, where Souci and Black Basile would be able to brag about their adventures up on the Barren Grounds. Guy headed south to Fort Smith and home to Ottawa, with a vision of the North firmly fixed in his mind, and already planning his next expedition.

FOUR — EXPLORATION: 1924–1925

From the time Guy first became involved with surveying, his life had followed a pattern of periods as long as eighteen months at a time, living in a tent and eating cookhouse meals, with a few months back in Edmonton or Ottawa waiting for a new assignment. After receiving his commission as a Dominion Land Surveyor in 1910 he had been in charge of large survey parties, and his reputation for competence and fairness had grown steadily. Even after his marriage in 1914, as his work took him ever farther north, he was away for long stretches followed by several months in his own comfortable home at #110 Frank Street, in Ottawa, not far from the Rideau Canal.[1]

Apart from one holiday at the Lake of the Woods in Ontario in 1915, Guy and Eileen had never been able to spend a summer together.[2] Perhaps to compensate for this, in the spring of 1924 they sailed to England for a touring holiday. While there, they hoped to see John Hornby who had sometimes visited their home in Ottawa after his meeting with Guy on Great Slave Lake. While visiting the scenic Vale of Evesham in Worcestershire, they received a letter from Hornby explaining that he was uncertain of being able to meet them as planned because he could not leave his aging parents.[3] Hornby's home at Nantwich was only a few miles from the railway junction point at Crewe, and in the end he and his mother arranged to join Guy and Eileen there on the boat train to Liverpool and see them off on the ship to Canada. Mrs. Hornby took the opportunity to beg Guy to persuade her son to stay home in England where he was needed, and by the time they sailed Guy thought he had succeeded in putting her case to Hornby.

Back in Canada, Guy immediately plunged into preparations for his return to the North. He had elaborate plans to survey the area he had explored briefly the previous summer with Souci and Black Basile, but this time he would have the company of two other surveyors, each with full crews. One of the surveyors, John Russell, had gone ahead early in the spring to complete the last part of the survey of the north arm of Great Slave Lake, using a dog team to cross the ice, and Guy would time his arrival in the North to coincide with the ice going out.

On this and succeeding trips when he was beyond any contact with a postal service, Guy kept a diary, which was in effect a long letter to his wife. The 1924 diary begins with the words, "It is rather funny the feeling I have that it is perhaps the last of my long trips into this country."[4] That is a strange comment from a man who would continue making long trips into the North for at least twenty more years. It may have been prompted by a close call he had at the beginning of the trip.[5]

Before the major survey trip could begin, Guy had to collect John Russell from somewhere on the north shore of Great Slave Lake. Sailing the *Ptarmigan* with a skeleton crew from Fort Resolution where she had wintered, Guy followed the south shore of Great Slave Lake around to the entrance to the Mackenzie River, and continued on to Hardisty Island at the western side of the north arm where he found John Russell waiting for him. With low misty clouds dimming the horizon, a rising northeast wind and poor anchorage on the island, they quickly loaded the ten men, ten dogs, canoe, toboggan and gear on board, setting off to cross the sixty miles of the lake without delay. It was ten o'clock at night when they launched the boat. With a ten-hour crossing ahead of them, they needed good light to navigate the shoals around Fort Resolution. The dogs, chained on deck to keep them apart, had all been fed and were soon seasick with the rising sea. Guy found that the pile of gear on deck had affected the ship's compass, so from time to time during the crossing he climbed to the cabin roof to take bearings on light spots in the cloud cover using a hand-held compass. It was a miserable night and the men had all sought shelter in the cabin and were soon asleep, leaving only Guy and the dog watcher on deck, bundled up against the chill and wearing oilskins.

About midnight, Guy went forward to take another sighting with the compass, and as he was climbing to the cabin roof, a big wave struck the boat. He lost his balance and was thrown overboard. Fortunately the dog watcher heard the splash and noted in his mind its direction. But many moments elapsed before the engine could be stopped and the other men roused. As well, the canoe had to be disentangled from the dog chains and the other equipment on deck before it could be launched.

Even though Guy was a good swimmer, he was wearing too many clothes to make any headway in the water and could only just keep his head above water. The icy cold penetrated quickly, cramps were coming on and his situation seemed hopeless. Just as he was resigning himself to his fate, he heard voices and the sound of paddles. He had not wasted his breath in shouting against the wind, but now he called out, "You'd better hurry." As he was close to losing consciousness, he felt someone grab his wrist and pull him into the canoe. Once safely back on board the *Ptarmigan* and rolled in blankets, his shivering and cramps gradually subsided and he fell asleep. Several hours later he woke in broad daylight, recollected what had happened, and realized with a start that no one on board knew the coast they were approaching and the danger of shoals ahead. He threw off the blankets and dashed up on deck, astonishing the steersman, who, without knowing it, was heading straight for the mud banks of the delta of the Slave River. Guy was able to correct the course just in time, and they landed safely, none the worse for his misadventure.

Guy began his diary for Eileen with the words foreshadowing the end of his northern travels soon after recovering from this accident, by which time the remaining members of the survey crew had arrived in the North and were on board the *Ptarmigan*. With seven canoes in tow and five tons of baggage, they were held up for two days by a storm in the Jean Marie Channel, the most easterly channel through the Slave River delta. While waiting there, they witnessed the arrival of a straggling fleet of large and small canoes, crowded with people,

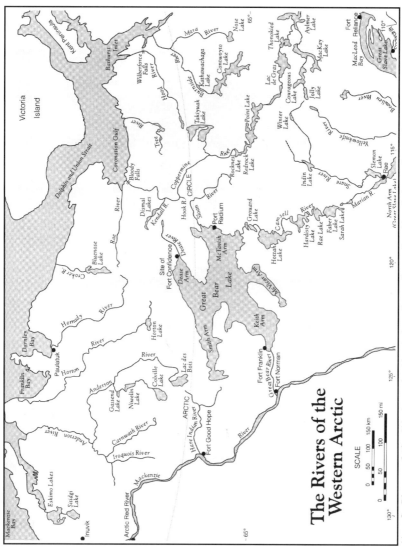

Map 3. Rivers of the Western Arctic, taken from *Canoeing North into the Unknown*, 167.

dogs and gear, headed for the annual distribution of treaty money at Fort Resolution. As Guy watched them paddling in with the late sunset behind them, he could imagine he was watching a scene of Native life from long ago.[6]

It was late June and ice still blocked their way beyond the narrow strait into the eastern end of Great Slave Lake where again they were delayed as they waited for a north wind to clear the passage. Guy had made elaborate plans for the work ahead, and was so aware of the limited time in which to do it that he hid his depression from the others by immersing himself in a book. He had brought along two books of Russian short stories, one of Irish folklore, but the one that gave him the most pleasure was *The Diary of Samuel Pepys*, with its lively tales of seventeenth-century London.

At last they reached the harbour where the schooner would be left at the eastern tip of Great Slave Lake, near Fort Reliance, and began the five-mile carry up 700 feet at the beginning of Pike's Portage. Even with a set of wheels for the canoes, it took six trips of heavy packing to get the rest of the baggage up and over the portage, and it was July 11 before the canoes were launched on Artillery Lake. Here the three survey parties split up, agreeing to meet on the same spot on the first of September. Max Cameron would go east and north investigating the land toward the Thelon and Back rivers, while John Russell would go west to survey the lakes on the plateau north of Great Slave Lake. Guy's objective was to find and map the source of the Coppermine River, and for this he would go straight through Artillery and Clinton-Colden lakes to begin his work at the entrance to Aylmer Lake which he had seen the previous year with Souci and Black Basile. In his diary he wrote, "Always a pleasurable thrill in slipping off into the unknown, especially here where the map is such a blank."

Near the end of Clinton-Colden Lake a storm forced them to take shelter and when it had abated they met an ice field which took a day to pass. At the Strait of Thanakoia Guy camped on the last familiar ground — from here on he would be exploring waters unknown to him. At the north end of Aylmer Lake, at the portage leading to Sussex Lake, they found a cairn containing a caribou antler inscribed "E.T. Seton, 10 Aug. 1907."[7] After surveying the perimeter of Aylmer Lake, they crossed its southern expanse and entered the Outram or upper Lockhart River. To find his way, Guy was using descriptions of the country by Warburton Pike, and also by James Stewart and James Anderson[8] in 1855, on their way to the Arctic coast to search for Franklin. The Native people had told him there would be no rapids on the Outram River, but soon after entering it they encountered heavy rapids leading to a sizeable lake — really a lake expansion of the Lockhart River — set between high parallel ridges. They assumed, wrongly as it happened, that this was MacKay Lake, and that they should strike off to the northwest to find the Coppermine.

It was now July 24, and the season for exploring was half over. A short reconnaissance to the north showed them country well supplied with lakes enclosed by a range of blue hills, with a notch on the northern horizon. Preparing to make long portages, they cached most of their outfit at the Outram River, taking with them a small canoe, a silk tent, light bedding, a rifle, ammunition, fishing tackle, tea, sugar and salt, and several roasting sticks, expecting to live off the country. For two days they worked their way slowly northward, numerous small lakes breaking the monotony of portaging. Twice unexpected passes let them through a forbidding range of hills. Finally, they crossed a low divide and launched the canoe on a large lake enclosed by hills. From its situation and character they thought it might be the Lac de Gras they had been told about. But after two days travel they reached its western extremity and finding a river flowing *into* the lake instead of out of it, they knew it was not that particular body of water. Guy later named it Thonokied Lake, from the description in Hearne's travel account.

The weather became stormy, fuel was scarce — and worse still — the caribou had deserted them. Once again they climbed a hill to view the land and seeing a sheet of water on the western horizon, they prepared for a long portage. During the night a gathering storm forced them to camp without good shelter, and as the storm increased in violence, the gale snapped their tent pole. There would be no replacement until they returned to the treeline. Becoming

Courtesy of Richard Blanchet

Guy Blanchet, centre of canoe, with survey crew on Lac de Gras, 1924.

soaked by the driving rain, they moved to shelter behind a huge boulder in a protected hollow, driving out two caribou that had sought shelter there before them. The storm abated by noon the next day, the caribou migration arrived, and they took time to cook a meal and dry their soaked clothes and bedding, before setting out again toward the big lake.

Guy, going ahead of his two companions, shot a caribou and cached it before heading back to assist in the portage, but when they arrived at the cache they met three white wolves just finishing off the remains of the meat. The migration had now passed and as they continued west on the big lake, there was not a caribou to be seen. On the third day of August they reached the big lake, which Guy felt confident was the Lac de Gras that Souci Beaulieu had described to him. They entered from the northeast and saw the lake opening out in a series of confusing bays to the south. Determined not to miss any clues, they investigated each bay, swinging south and then west, but in each case only small streams flowed into — not out of — the lake. As the little canoe beat its way westward against the wind, it was necessary to lighten it by having one man walk along the shore.

The stormy weather and the lack of caribou made it an anxious journey around the lake, and as they approached the west end of the lake it appeared to be enclosed by high hills. Only when examining the last possible bay did they hear the distant roar

Courtesy of Janet Blanchet

Guy Blanchet and the cairn at the beginning of the Coppermine River, 1924. "The Arctic was only 100 miles away, but summer was passed and we had a paddle of 400 miles back to the schooner, so here we turned homeward."

of a heavy rapid and by climbing into the hills could see a river tumbling through a succession of rapids and then emerging onto a fine open plain. At last they had found the Coppermine River. The Arctic was only 100 miles away, but mid-summer had passed and there was a paddle of 400 miles yet required to complete their survey and reach the *Ptarmigan*.

They built a cairn, left a record of the exploration in it, and then proceeded to work their way back around the north side of the lake, through Lake Paul and Lac du Sauvage, where they saw the upper Coppermine River enter the lake. Fortunately, on the north side of the lake they met the caribou again and their supply problems were over. Proceeding south the way they had come, they returned to the point where they had cached the bulk of their outfit, and continued up the Outram River. Portaging past a thirty-foot cascade of water, and more continuous rapids, they reached MacKay Lake, which proved to be more than 100 feet above Aylmer Lake. They explored the full extent of MacKay and found it was long and sinuous and located in quite a different place than had been shown on previous maps.

In his diary at the Coppermine River, Guy had written, "I was just sketching our travel on the map and it looks woefully small, however it represents something definite, which means a lot in this country." When the three survey parties finally met at the beginning of September on Artillery Lake, they had the geographical details to map an area of well over 100 miles square encompassing all of the Lockhart River basin.

Guy and his two companions were first to arrive at the bottom of Pike's Portage, and canoed around to Fort Reliance to get the *Ptarmigan*, which had been in harbour there all summer. As their canoes touched the shore, they were greeted by John Hornby who had just finished building a cache and was preparing to head up the portage with a group of trappers to spend the winter in the area just above Artillery Lake. With Hornby was J.C. Critchell-Bullock, a British ex-cavalry officer, who had left the army after contracting malaria in India and had come to find new experiences in the Canadian North and restore his health. Over six feet tall and with an aristocratic bearing, he was a complete contrast to the man who had taken him on as a partner for a winter of trapping and living off the land.

Blanchet and Hornby, who had parted company earlier that year on the steamship dock in Liverpool, were glad to see each other and spent some time talking about the portage, the caribou and the wolves in the area Guy had just left. Small, wiry and strong, the two men had more in common than their size and their ability to pack close to their own weight over a portage. Both shared a mystical love of the wide open northland, enjoyed the challenge of surviving off the land and welcomed the contacts with the Native people. But where Hornby was a loner who often lived hand-to-mouth without plan or obvious purpose, Blanchet was disciplined, orderly, careful about the safety of those working under him. He was a capable leader who enjoyed congenial company, but if he found nothing in common with the men in his crew he was able to withdraw into himself and be aloof from them.

Despite his often unkempt appearance, Hornby had some vanity. When they met, Guy was sporting two-months growth of whiskers, having just come off a long trip on the Barrens. Hornby, seeing the effect of a beard on his friend's appearance, immediately dashed off to his shack and shaved.[9]

As pre-arranged, Hornby bought five canoes and some gear from Blanchet, and the next day Guy transported Hornby and his party to the beginning of Pike's Portage on the *Ptarmigan*. There he met the rest of the survey party as they came off the portage, and with everything loaded aboard the *Ptarmigan*, they set off for Fort Resolution and the south.

That fall, the chairman of the Geographic Board of Canada recommended Guy to be a Fellow of the Royal Geographic Society — the prestigious body in London to which most outstanding explorers belong. From December of that year, the initials FRGS began to appear behind his name on publications.[10]

In spite of the prediction at the beginning of his 1924 trip that it might be his last long journey into the north, in June of 1925 Guy was back in Fitzgerald on the Slave River ready to strike off into a new area of unmapped country for the Topographical Survey. In his mind he was following a route mapped out by Dr. Richard King, the medical officer on George Back's expedition in 1834. King had noted that late breakup of the ice on the large lakes always delayed travel to the Arctic on the regularly accepted route, and had produced a map based on information from the Natives, which began in the country southeast of Great Slave Lake. When there was anxiety about the missing Franklin expedition in 1847, King urged the use of the inland route in the search, but his idea was dismissed as impractical and was never used. The route used a largely forgotten Native portage route between portions of two large rivers. Guy was about to set off with a crew of three to discover the truth of this map, and survey the area to map it accurately.[11]

The journey would be into the land of the Chipweyan or "Caribou Eaters," and Guy set about learning as much as possible about the country from the Natives at Fitzgerald. They described the route up the Taltson River to a big lake, two hundred miles long, which reached out into the Barrens, but their travel was usually in winter following the caribou. They assured him it could not be done by canoe and none

Courtesy of Richard Blanchet

Guy and Jack showing the limitations of the folding canoe, 1925.

was willing to go along as a guide, until at the last moment two were persuaded to show them the beginning of the route.

As usual at the start of a long trek into the unknown, Guy had mixed feelings. After a few days out, looking at the trail ahead with long views in the sunset, part of him was stirred by the "primitive love of travel and trails," while the other part was filled with thoughts of his wife and home and the pleasant times left behind. At the beginning of the trip, his companions, Tom Wallis, a strong, willing, university student, and Albert, a Métis who had travelled into the interior, were still unknown quantities, while Jack, the steersman had been with him before. He was pleased to find that Tom had an interest in old civilizations, giving the prospect of some congenial conversation.

Using only one nineteen-foot Peterborough canoe, they also carried a small, folding canvas boat. When the four men, their surveying instruments and essential equipment were loaded into the canoe, there was very little room left for supplies. Guy chose to leave behind bacon and a sack of flour, pinning his faith on eighty pounds of buffalo pemmican. "It takes about forty pounds of fish a day to feed us…we must reach the caribou next month or fall back on fresh supplies somewhere…wouldn't mind if we had to starve a little to see what the mental reaction would be."

Along with the two Native guides in their own canoe, they left Fitzgerald on June 11 and started up the river, the old route up to the plateau leading to the interior. The Dog River gradually dwindled to nothing and they portaged across to the Tethul River, continuing upstream until it became too small for the large canoe to navigate, and once again they portaged up through lightly wooded country with a scattering of small lakes until they reached the much larger Taltson River, a river that flows through a series of lake expansions connected by cataracts and gorges. Once they had reached the first of these lakes, the Natives expressed the wish to leave them — they had gone beyond their knowledge of the land and had a thousand reasons why they were needed at home. Since they were also consuming quantities of the limited supplies, Guy gave them permission to turn back.

The group had now gone beyond the existing maps, and when river bends hid the view the only way to plot the future direction was to climb up the sides of the gorge and look at the terrain. After two weeks and many miles of travel they reached the long lake, which they had been told at Fitzgerald was the traditional route for the muskox hunters to reach the Thelon River. This was Nonacho — or Big Point — Lake, a great sprawling body of water that stretched for nearly 100 miles in a confusion of bays and channels, making it a challenge to map. After such hard steady travel Guy chose to treat Sunday as a rest day, and used it to catch up with his notes to work out their position and think about the route ahead.

His diary took the form of a long, continuous letter to his wife, Eileen, that she could read when he returned home, and where, along with describing the trip day by day, he occasionally expressed his deeper feelings: "I have an air that runs through my head when we are travelling made up of all the sadness of a lonely trail at evening and far, far views in the sunset, and still I like it — it seems to stir up some primitive love of travel and trails." And a few days later: "This is one of the blue times — the lake has pushed out to three straggling arms running into the hills and holding the wrong direction...Things get so bad, if you persevere they usually break well. Just as I was deciding to portage, some piled stones led us to a small break and passing it, a big open sea that was hidden by hills last night." In his diary he continued to muse on the nature of being an explorer, the need to think more of the work than of himself, ignoring wet and cold, fly bites and fatigue. He found it easy to relate to the primitive mind for whom the world is bounded by the horizon, and speculation is reduced to imagination and superstition. However, when his calculations were completed he found the day in camp long and tedious and had to use patience to restrain his anxious thoughts about the trail ahead.

The four men worked well together, forming a contented party that enjoyed serious talks as well as jokes, willing to plug ahead cheerfully confident that they would find their way in the end, even though after three weeks the estimated position showed them to be in the middle of nowhere, and with very little food left. For a time the travel had been pleasant. An abundance of fish eased their supply problems and camping was in beautiful country marked with caribou trails, in clean groves of spruce and jackpine beside wide beaches. Each bend brought enough variety in the scene to hold their interest. Always there was evidence of the people, the "Caribou Eaters" who had lived and hunted on this land in the recent and distant past. Portaging around a falls, Guy found a toy boat, whittled from a stick, and pictured the "little brown tot, caribou grease to the ears, sailing it on the eddy below the falls."

In searching for the headwaters of the Thelon River, they had been told that they should keep to the left when they reached a fork, but in country without distinguishing features, it was hard to know at which fork this advice was intended. Where Nonacho Lake branched they had gone to the east and were still going up the Taltson River, portaging past heavy rapids and enduring the fierce onslaught of the mosquitoes.[12]

As long as they were following the Taltson upstream and through its lake expansions, they felt they were on the right track, but as the river constricted and turned in an unexpected direction

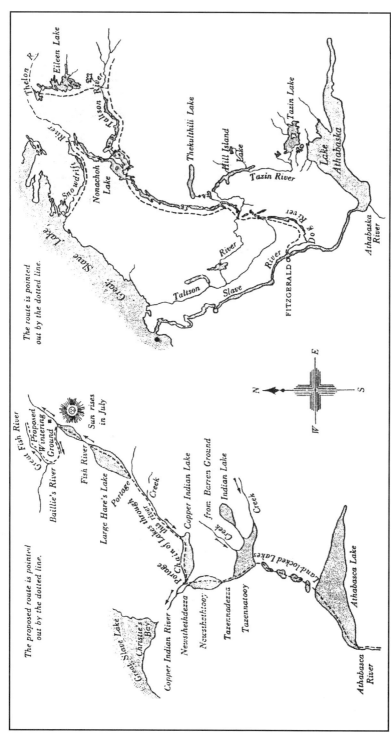

Map 4. Maps of the canoe route followed by Guy Blanchet. Map on the left drawn by Guy Blanchet. Map on the right possibly drawn by Dr. Richard King; map on the right possibly drawn by Blanchet, taken from the Canadian Field-Naturalist, April 1962, 70.

they had to stop and take stock. Modern topographical maps of the area show an undulating land with small lakes and tiny ponds, meandering streams and the occasional bog, giving an idea of the kind of territory they were exploring, using only hearsay directions, their intuition and the information they could glean by climbing the highest points of land. By July 8 the river had become almost a continuous rapid. Using the canvas folding canoe, Guy set off with one of the men, Jack, to explore ahead but found the river and country unnavigable and returned to the base camp.

His diary, written in pencil on lined paper in small notebooks of a size that could tuck easily into his pack, is a good reflection of their situation. "Shall move back to last lake and south, we thought we saw a river come in there. The situation is blue. The country is miserable for cross-country travel. Prepared to do any reasonable amount of work to get through, but it would be folly to start heavy portaging along a route we weren't certain came through to the Thelon."

It is possible that they were on a dead-end lake expansion of the Taltson River at the point where the river turns south when Guy wrote:

> Away up the lake — the unexplored N.E. fork. Taking the afternoon off. It is very hot with little wind and in the morning all of us shall start overland intending to go till we find something definite. This year at first it was hard to put my heart into it. Well now it [my heart] is and I shall be terribly disappointed if I couldn't make it. Nobody except ourselves thought we could. Only McDougall at Ft. Smith said the trip was a possible one. The boys are willing to work their heads off and live on tripe de roche if necessary to get through, and rely on me to find the way. I can't take too big chances either of getting lost or grub shortage. I should go back with a much lighter heart if I could succeed. Finished Dante's Inferno yesterday.

Three days of exploration in intense heat yielded nothing, and they backtracked to the larger lake expansion of the Taltson, now called Grey Lake. The next plan was for Guy and Jack to set out with the folding canoe and the lightest possible outfit, going northeast. Using the canoe on small lakes and much portaging in the chosen direction, they climbed the bare hills to look ahead, and on one they found piled stones which they took to be a sign marking an old route. Toward the end of their second day they reached a big lake that seemed to stretch into the north and east, with clean open hills and beaches of sand and gravel. The folding canoe had limitations on the open lake and they were windbound for a day on a point, but they had begun to catch large trout and their starving time was over. Feeling cheerful and hopeful, Guy named the lake, Eileen Lake, for his wife.

They explored Eileen Lake thoroughly, surveying and mapping the deep bays and islands, always hoping to find a river flowing out. Five days from the time they left the base camp they came to a heavy rapid at the beginning of the northern bay of the lake. Guy optimistically believed he had found the Thelon River, even though the river was flowing northwest. They explored as far as they dared, built a cairn and left a record, concerned that they were now forty miles from the base camp. With only tea and sugar left, they were dependent on the fish they could catch. What was even more serious, they were almost out of tobacco. By this time, Guy had pretty well memorized the only book he had carried with him, *The Rubyiat*, by Omar Khayyam, and found it a perfect expression of his own thoughts.

Eleven days after leaving they arrived back at the base camp, finding that the two men who remained behind had decided twice that Guy and Jack were lost, first after reckoning their supplies were exhausted, and the second time when they were sure they would be out of tobacco.

Guy's initial plan on setting out had been to follow the Thelon River to its confluence with the Hanbury, and return up the Hanbury and out via Artillery Lake and Pike's Portage. The season was now too far advanced to consider such a trip, but to return the

Courtesy of Richard Blanchet

The Snowdrift River on its way to "fall down the mountain," 1925.

way they had come would offer no real interest or accomplishment. With a freshly shot moose providing the first meal of fresh meat of the summer, they preserved the rest as best they could, broke camp and started back to Nonacho Lake, heading this time for the northern branch of the lake, hoping it would take them out to the Snowdrift River.

As they entered Nonacho Lake they came to a camp of Chipweyan, heading in the direction from which they had just come, and stopped to talk as best they could through one member of the survey party who spoke a little of the language. The Chipweyan had limited knowledge of the country, with the exception of a blind woman who was about ninety years old and who became very animated on hearing them ask about the Thelon River and the Barren Lands. She had been far to the east with her people as a young girl, had seen the river, crossed the Barrens and wintered on a lake at the edge of the forest, which Guy understood to be Artillery Lake. She described the route to her son who drew a map that matched the route they had been following. This encounter with the people whose way of life was to follow the caribou thrilled Guy, who was always watching for signs left by their ancestors.

Continuing up Nonacho Lake they met a second group of Chipweyan and asked them about the Snowdrift River. The Natives told of long and difficult portages and drew a map for them, warning the survey party to leave the river before it fell down the mountain. At the end of Noman Lake, the surveyors picked their way over rough, rocky ground, through rugged hills over the portage route that had been described, carrying their heavy canoe and gear. The reward came at the summit where they looked out over an extensive valley and saw the Snowdrift River meandering through park-like groves of trees, the white sand beaches along the river giving rise to the name of Snowdrift.

The river travel began with long stretches of easy current and occasional rapids where boulder moraine crossed the valley, and they took time to map the course of the river as they went. There were five days of pleasant travel, but Guy's mind was more disturbed than the river, knowing they had to drop 600 feet to reach the level of Great Slave Lake, and remembering the Indian description of "falling down the mountain." They were running short of meat and there were few fish in the river. As Guy wrote in the June 1950 issue of *The Beaver*:

> The valley closed in and the river cut sharply into the mountains. As we entered a moderate rapid, the head of a bear appeared above the bushes. A shot from the bouncing canoe secured a much needed supply of meat. But looking back, the gap in the mountains appeared as a gate closing behind us. We were committed to "fall down the mountain," or to abandon the canoe and travel overland with our folding canoe.

They dropped 500 feet in six miles and spent three days making that distance, with the roar of the water reverberating in their ears as they passed between high vertical walls from which there was no escape.

It was a huge relief when they emerged safely on to the peaceful water and familiar view of Great Slave Lake.

They met the advance guard of Yellowknife heading out to hunt caribou. Among them was an old man with whom Guy had once travelled. He asked by what road they had reached the lake, and when Guy told him they had followed the river down the mountain, he shook his head gravely and said, "I think maybe no."

Looking back on the trip, Guy wrote in his diary:

> It seems a strange wandering, always lured on by a distant view or the hope of new waters, meeting failure sometimes but success remarkably often. We have travelled 600 miles, and even the old travellers did not have a more blank map to work on, and they usually had Indian guides. The personal equation is everything on a trip like this with nothing to control or drive it. The amount of work we do in a day depends on what I think is right, and no one could complain as our day starts before 6 and seldom ends before 9. The party has been splendid — all working well and keen cheerfulness prevails. They have a blind confidence in my pulling things through.

After the usual route back up the Slave/Athabasca River, the train from Waterways to Edmonton, and from Edmonton to Ottawa, Guy gave a talk to the Canadian Field Naturalists in Ottawa during the winter. He described finding the source of the Thelon River, but by the time it was published in April/May 1926 he knew that the river he had found was not the Thelon, and once more the following spring would find him heading to the North to complete his search.

FIVE — THE LAST EXPLORATION
ON THE BARRENS: 1926

Knowing that John Hornby and James Critchell-Bullock were setting off to spend the winter trapping in the vicinity of Casba — or as it is now called, Ptarmigan — Lake, just beyond Artillery Lake, and also knowing of Hornby's abilities to live and travel in the North, Guy had suggested to O.S. Finnie, director of the Northwest Territories and Yukon Branch of the Canadian government, that his friend be hired to make a survey of wildlife on the Barrens.[1] To assist the enterprise, Guy had not only brought in the supplies for the Hornby-Bullock trip but had also transported the party from Fort Reliance to the beginning of Pike's Portage when they were heading north in 1924.

Hornby and Critchell-Bullock spent a miserably uncomfortable winter living in a cave excavated from an esker just beyond the treeline, trapping, hunting game for the cooking pot and collecting specimens of wildlife. The circumstances are fully described in the book *Snow Man* by Malcolm Waldron, based on the diaries of Critchell-Bullock, and in a chapter of *The Legend of John Hornby* by George Whalley. Using his personal knowledge of both the men and the territory, Guy, thirty years later, wrote a quixotic story "The Letter," which appeared in the spring issue of *The Beaver* in 1963. In four short pages and using fictional technique, he brilliantly recreated the tensions that built up between the two men over the winter when each thought the other was mad. In brief, here are a few paragraphs that give the gist of the story:

"See here, Bullock, you get many letters and no one

> *writes to me. I'll give you five pounds, one fox skin, for*
> *one of your letters in the next mail."*

In a moment of despair Bullock had written to the police at the nearest post to say that he thought that Hornby was insane and might become dangerous. Hornby returned from a prolonged trip with a packet of letters.

> *He dumped a packet of twenty or more on the floor and*
> *glanced at the addresses. "None for me, not one, but*
> *remember our bargain?"*
>
> *Hornby laughed as he carelessly picked out a long*
> *official envelope with RCMP stamped on the flap and*
> *shoved it in his pocket. "Not that one," Bullock cried,*
> *"that's private business."*

As the winter dragged on the friction between the two men increased. Hearing that Hornby had met Corporal Thorp of the RCMP on patrol when he was visiting his trapper friends, Bullock anxiously asked what he was after. Bullock became increasingly agitated in the days that followed as he thought Hornby was hiding something from him. Eventually, when they were both in a cheerful mood, Bullock got up his courage.

> *"I say, Jack," he tried to make it sound casual, "How*
> *about that letter."*
>
> *"Letter! What letter?" Hornby seemed to have no*
> *recollection of it.*
>
> *"You know well enough. The letter you bought for a*
> *fox skin. The police letter. The cursed letter."*
>
> *Hornby looked astonished, then burst out laughing.*
> *"Oh, now I remember. Surely that did not worry you?*
> *Here just a minute."*
>
> *From the pocket of an old pair of pants he produced*
> *a dirty, crumpled letter. It was unopened.*
>
> *Bullock tore the envelope open and drew out a*

thin, official slip and read: "Received from George Critchell-Bullock — the sum of Thirty dollars — for Licence to trap foxes in the Northwest Territories. Signed Corp. Thorp RCMP."

After the spring breakup, Hornby and Bullock set off and travelled out by canoe down the Thelon River to Baker Lake and on to Chesterfield Inlet, where they found a ship to take them to northern Quebec and another ship to Newfoundland. They finally reached Ottawa late in November 1925 with a huge story to tell, and in celebration Hornby invited Guy and Eileen to dinner at the Chateau Laurier, along with Critchell-Bullock. The Blanchets dressed appropriately, Bullock wore formal attire, while Hornby was his usual non-descript self. Bullock, in his best English upper-class manner, sent the waiter to question the chef and generally acted as host, and at the end of the meal Hornby was delighted when the waiter presented Bullock with the bill.[2]

Hornby immersed himself in writing a report for the government department describing what they had seen of the wildlife on their journey down the Thelon, and recommending that the government establish a game preserve in the area to safeguard the muskox and the wintering grounds of the caribou. He finished his report in less than two weeks, anxious to leave for England having heard that his father was critically ill.[3]

Critchell-Bullock stayed on in Ottawa working on his own report for the government department and finished it late in March. He rented an apartment across the canal from Guy and Eileen's home in the centre of the city and a firm friendship developed between them through the winter of 1926. Bullock had kept a regular diary and meticulous notes of his whole time in the North from which he wrote a lengthy article on many facets of the subject, published over a six-month period in the *Canadian Field-Naturalist* in 1930. While the northern trip was intended to be a partnership between Bullock and Hornby, Bullock had financed it and he was now running out of money and trying to get government backing to make another trip into the North — anything to put money into his bank account. Guy offered him a place on his survey crew, which would be heading north later in the spring, but Bullock turned it down because of a back injury, and headed off to the States where he eventually found work.[4]

By the beginning of May 1926, John Hornby was back in Ottawa from England with Edgar Christian, the son of his cousin,

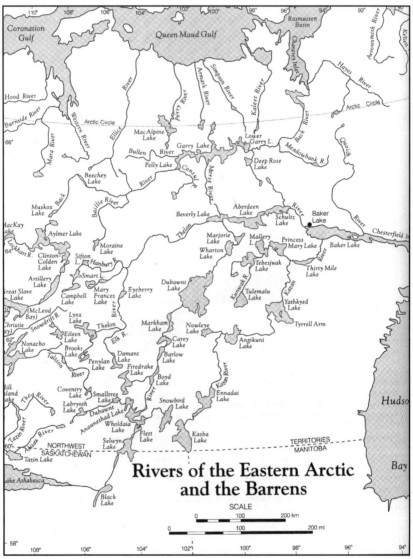

Map 5. Rivers of the Eastern Arctic and the Barrens, taken from Canoeing North into the Unknown, *100.*

a young man in his late teens, who would be accompanying him on his next trip into the North. Hornby had already cabled Blanchet from England with an outline of his plans hoping that he would once again help to transport Hornby's heavy gear to the Great Slave Lake area. The plan was to winter on a tree-studded section of the Thelon River that Hornby had seen the previous year. When Guy met Hornby's trusting and inexperienced young cousin in Ottawa, he used every reasonable argument to try to dissuade them from going, but without success.[5]

They would meet again toward the end of May in Edmonton, where Guy was putting together the outfit for his next survey trip. Again Guy was unable to convince Hornby not to take Edgar to winter on the Barrens. Soon after, Hornby and Edgar Christian were joined by another young Englishman, Harold Adlard, and all three left on the train for Waterways to begin canoeing down the Athabasca River, along with Jack McDermot who had been hired by Blanchet for his survey. When Guy met them at Fort Chipewyan a few days later, he made a final effort to change Hornby's plans by offering to employ him along with Edgar Christian on the survey to search for the headwaters of the Thelon, but since there were now three in Hornby's party and Guy had only space for two, Hornby would not accept.[6] Guy watched them leave down the Slave River with a sense of foreboding. John Hornby had miraculously survived starvation more than once in the North, sometimes with the help of Native people in the area, but this time he had chosen an area where no one lived and few, if any, trapped and he had in his care two young "greenhorns" with no experience at all.[7]

By the end of the first week of June, Guy had two of his crew members, Jack McDermot and Aimé, a man strong, capable and experienced on surveys, but with a quick temper that could turn nasty. They travelled east on Lake Athabasca in a gas-powered boat to Black Bay, the most northerly point of the lake, to the beginning of the Camsell Portage. The portage up onto the plateau, 250 feet above the lake, was a test of muscle and stamina at the beginning of the season. It was Jack's first time packing over a portage and he felt his lack of wind, as did Guy, carrying a load of 120 pounds.[8]

As they headed up to Tazin Lake, they met a party of Chipewyan coming down from their winter trapping on the way out to the annual summer gathering at Fort Chipewyan. Guy engaged them in talk to learn as much as he could about the country they had just left, and to try to persuade one to come along as a guide, but their feeling was that the summer was a time for pleasant gatherings and not for hard travel over tough portages. They told him that from the headwaters of the Tazin River they would reach another river flowing northeast, which had a name meaning "skin of an animal." After a couple of days of parlay, Zachary Ledouceur agreed to come along and make the whole trip with them. He appeared strong, lazy and dull, but brightened up when Guy talked to him in Cree.

For a week they made their way up the new river, now named the Abitau, climbing steadily upward, portaging past many rapids and a heavy waterfall. At times the river became difficult to follow, sometimes dammed by eskers and moraines and with many choices of route, none of them obvious. They were on a rising plateau in headwater country of a particularly difficult kind, often stumbling over rough or swampy portages with heavy loads, always plagued by biting flies.

Blanchet using the wireless for the time signal to establish longitude on the Abitau River, 1926.

Guy's diary written for his wife gives full rein to his feelings: "It is unfortunate that the men control so much of the enjoyment of a trip like this, and the right kind are almost impossible to get. From the indications I am afraid it is going to be a case of withdrawing to write or read. I don't think I will take a long trip again — too hard on one's spirit to live in an uncongenial atmosphere month after month — makes it hard for me to get used to people in the fall. Will call on my philosophy and remember time passes quickly and the mists and storms are soon forgotten. Ten years ago I wouldn't have considered a summer holiday in preference to the trail — but I have changed. When I look back to our pleasure in just a canoe trip or a walk or golf, it makes me feel I am missing too much."

At the same time Guy felt guilty of mental snobbery with his "odd rambling mind and different scale of values." The best times were when all were working hard and moving forward, even when the going was tough. And Guy did work hard on these trips. On a typical morning he was up at 5:30 to light the fire and put the pots on to boil, while the other men rolled their beds. As the men cooked, he rolled his bed and took down the tent. After breakfast he washed the dishes and Jack dried, they packed and the other men lifted the packs, loaded the canoe. They were away just over an hour later.

The barometer showed they had reached 1,700 feet above sea level, 400 feet more than the known general height of the plateau, and were on a great dome-shaped area where there were no indications of the direction to follow. The small portable wireless, essential for accurate time checks, was not working, and he had to take a sighting of Polaris, the North Star, to work out the longitude. With the river petering out, Guy took Zachary and a small stock of pemmican and headed north to look for the route. Almost immediately they plunged into muskeg, broken at intervals by low rock ridges and stretches of sand hills. Little streams flowed in various directions and while it was difficult to find the route, Guy found it intensely interesting to study the drainage. Finally they found a stream flowing east, traced it on through two lakes until it became a decent size, and saw the country sloping downward to the northeast.

They had abandoned the canoe twelve miles back, and having now found a river flowing in the right direction, they started back to pick up the canoe and the rest of the party. Their way was barred by narrow sections of dangerous floating bogs, and as they detoured around occasional lakes the route became obscure, and they finally stopped for the night. While Zachary covered his head with a piece of canvas to keep off the bugs and slept, Guy watched the sun dip below the horizon and the light change through every delicate shade of the spectrum. He listened to the sounds of nesting birds, somewhat melancholy with the constant repetition of the same note, staying awake to be ready to move with the first light. At three in the morning they were on their way.

Finding themselves on a point at the narrows of a large lake, they built a raft to cross and continued southward, but for a time were disoriented by the confusing travel they had done and afraid they would have to retrace their steps through difficult country. They stopped to smoke a pipe, collected their thoughts and then agreed to push on, finally reaching their canoe. Soon the whole party was across the divide and Guy's spirits rose, believing he was on the beginnings of the Thelon River — his goal for the second summer in a row.

As the river gathered strength, the rapids increased but there was good teamwork with Aimé in the stern and Guy in the bow. In going through a heavier rapid than usual, when they had taken the precaution to take out half the load and two of the men, they had a moment of high excitement when the river swung sharply into a rocky gorge and the sound changed, warning them of a waterfall ahead. They managed to run the canoe up on a smooth rock and jump out before the river plunged over a drop of forty feet as it left a lake full of islands, which is now named Insula Lake.

The river led them into a lake of long narrow arms, each of which had to be searched for the outlet. Guy named it Labyrinth Lake, and in an article in *The Beaver*, September 1949, he identified it as the lake that Samuel Hearne called "Thelewey-aza-yeth," where he and his party had paused for ten days on their return from the Coppermine to Fort Churchill in 1772. Guy's reason for choosing this lake over others is that there were many good birch trees growing in the area that would have been used to make canoes for the journey, whereas the lakes of a similar shape to Hearne's description were too high on the plateau for trees to grow.

As the river continued east, the trip was turning into a nightmare of obstacles, blind bays, headwinds and rapids, as well as outbursts of temper from Aimé. Worse still, Guy was beginning to doubt that the river they were on was the Thelon and suspected they were headed for the Dubawnt, which did not interest him — it had already been mapped by Joseph Burr Tyrrell.[9] After explaining the situation to the crew, he volunteered to go ahead on foot for a day to determine where they were, and then if they wished to turn back he was willing, although it would be over difficult ground.

After a serious talk the men agreed to co-operate, Guy explored on and found a lake which he named Small Tree because of the light timber. Once he was back in the canoe with the crew, they had two more days of heavy rapids, which brought them to another lake, named Sunday for the day. There they searched fifty miles of shoreline looking for the outlet and finally found it. The outlet was hidden by a hill high enough to give the view of a large lake to the south — Wholdaia. This discovery finally confirmed that they were on the waters of the Dubawnt.

Courtesy of Richard Blanchet

Loaded for the last portages on the Dubawnt River, 1926.

Despite his disappointment in not finding the Thelon, Guy was encouraged by realizing the amount of empty territory he had mapped, but his diary for this year was full of introspection and self-examination. "Wish I were not so sensitive to the atmosphere about me. I sometimes look at Zachary, stolid, unthinking and good-humoured — little penetrates or disturbs him and nothing elates. A protective armour of sluggishness of mind and spirit saves him from much unnecessary care, while my spirit is naked and constantly battered about...When I work alone I can generally be cheerful — with the boys, the swearing, grumbling and bad humour depresses me more than work and hardships. Only Zachary has a face that lights up with a smile — he sings too, and we have little clumsy jokes in Cree...I always admit it must be myself who is out of step with the world." Even the books he carried that year were disappointing. The travels of Marco Polo had become tedious, and *Tristram Shandy*, one of the earliest English novels, lacked imagination, and he wished he had brought Pepys diaries instead.

Having again missed the Thelon, he found himself thinking he would make another trip the following year, because he hated to be defeated in his quest for a river. He resolved that on another such trip it would only be with Natives or with someone he knew he could enjoy. "It is a life for a man — everyday a fight, always facing decisions. No wonder I find the office wishy-washy, with its smug pretensions, little given or received."

The journey south to Selwyn Lake was straightforward, and then it was downhill all the way to Lake Athabasca where Guy hoped to find a power boat to take them back to Fort Chipewyan. The journey was finishing just after the middle of July, nearly two months early and he looked forward to getting home to his wife, remembering the holiday they had in Bermuda in the spring.

The diaries preserved in the archives are almost a one-way conversation in which Guy opens his heart and expresses his feelings to his wife. In some ways they are revealing, but they tell nothing of the life he shared with Eileen in Ottawa during the months that Guy was back from his northern explorations and working in the office of the Department of the Interior. While there is never any mention of the Blanchet family in his journals, it seems that he kept in touch with his mother and his siblings; his father had died in 1915.[10]

In Edmonton, on his way home, Guy met his youngest brother, Geoffrey, who had gone to the prairies to look for harvest work. Nothing in Geoffrey's life had prepared him for the work or the living conditions and, finding him distraught, Guy accompanied him home to Vancouver Island before returning to Ottawa.[11]

Clever and artistic, Geoffrey had started his career as a bank manager in Quebec and was promoted to be in charge of foreign exchange at the Toronto headquarters of the Bank of Commerce. His nervous, emotional temperament had caused a nervous breakdown when he was only in his forties and he took early retirement. With his wife, Muriel — later known as "Capi" — and their four children, he had driven west in 1922 in a Willys-Knight touring car, with flapping curtains and a fold-down top. It was no mean feat in those days of primitive highways, and they had to go south to Chicago to reach the west coast. On Vancouver Island they had found an enchanting English-style country cottage on seven acres of overgrown woodland looking toward the San Juan Islands, on a point of land east of Swartz Bay. Covered with ivy, the house had been empty for eight years when they bought it and moved in. At a nearby marina they had found a boat with a cabin and motor, *Caprice*, which had been built only the year before but had sunk at its mooring after being damaged by ice in the winter. They were able to buy it cheaply, repair it, and take the engine apart to clean it from its immersion in salt water. A fifth child was born some time after their arrival on the coast. The family had been living an idyllic life beside the sea.[12]

Guy had only just returned to Ottawa from Vancouver Island when word came that Geoffrey had gone off for a day of sailing by himself in *Caprice*. He had anchored and set up the stove for dinner, then disappeared without a trace. It was presumed that he had gone for a swim, had a heart attack and drowned, but his body was never found. While Capi was known to be clever and capable, her family and the Blanchet family were concerned about how she could manage with the five children on her own. It was arranged that the two oldest girls, Elizabeth and Frances, aged fifteen and thirteen, would live in Ottawa with Guy and Eileen, and attend school there.[13] This was a new experience for Guy and Eileen, with no children of their own to suddenly have a ready-made family of teenaged girls. They were only there for one year, going to Capi's family in Quebec the following year.

That year in Ottawa, Guy's work kept him in the office as he wrote up the report of his summer's work for the department and completed a comprehensive descriptive booklet, fully illustrated with photographs and maps, entitled *Great Slave Lake Area: Northwest Territories,* published by the government. This report outlined not only the surveys that had been done, but gave an overview of the geology and topography of the area, and contained chapters on settlement and transportation, climate and vegetation, the birds and animals to be found within the territory, as well as a bibliography of all that had been written about it, beginning with Samuel Hearne in 1795.

Guy enjoyed writing, and he also wrote an article about the journey just completed for the Geographical Society of Philadelphia, published in their *Bulletin* early in 1927. He had published the account of his previous year's trip in that journal the year before, and had written other articles about his northern surveys beginning with the *Canadian Field-Naturalist* in 1924, and the *Canadian Surveyor* in 1925.

Late in December 1926, Guy was surprised to receive a letter from Vilhjalmur Stefansson, who had heard of Guy's work from their mutual friend James Critchell-Bullock, whom he had met at the Explorers Club in New York. Stefansson suggested that they meet for lunch or dinner the next time Guy was in New York, so that he could hear the latest trends of opinion in Canada on the North, but in the meantime he requested a copy of Guy's latest article for the Geographical Society of Philadelphia. Flattered by Stefansson's interest, Guy sent off the requested article as well as the newly published official government report he had just completed. Stefansson's reply was complimentary, particularly about the report, and went on to suggest that since Guy had only seen the northern plains in summer he should have a couple of winters there to get a real feel for the country.[14] Despite his connection with two Arctic disasters, the loss of the *Karluk* and some of the scientific staff of the Canadian Arctic Expedition in 1914, and the death of four young men whom he had sent to establish British sovereignty on Wrangel Island in 1923, Stefansson, through his early expeditions to the Arctic and his books on the subject, was considered America's greatest expert on anything to do with the Arctic.

Replying to a New Year card from Stefansson early in January 1928, Guy expressed concern about the fate of their mutual friend, John Hornby, who had not been heard of since Guy watched him leave for the Thelon in spring of 1926. Guy described Hornby as "the most unselfish, impossible but lovable chap I have ever met," and added, with foreboding about the current circumstances, that Hornby "had gone in very light and rather hampered by two young chaps." Stefansson made light of Guy's concerns, writing that he had learned through Richard Finnie that there were no concerns about Hornby in official Ottawa. Stefansson suggested gratuitously that Blanchet or Critchell-Bullock should go in search of Hornby. Meanwhile, Critchell-Bullock was writing to Guy from the Explorers Club, "You are our only real travelling explorer today — I trust that you will bring back good news of Hornby."[15]

In Ottawa in the spring of 1927, Guy was introduced to George Douglas and his wife, Kay, from their home in Lakefield near Peterborough, by Dr. Charles Camsell, deputy minister of mines and resources. Camsell had been born at the fur trade post of Fort Simpson on the Mackenzie River. Douglas already knew and admired the published accounts of Blanchet's survey work around Great Slave Lake and was delighted to meet him face to face. It is most likely that Blanchet also knew Douglas's book, *Lands Forlorn*, about the year that Douglas, his brother Lionel, and geologist, Dr. August Sandberg, had spent in 1911 on Dease Bay in Great Bear Lake. The Douglas's returned to Ottawa the following spring and dined with the Blanchets at one of the Ottawa golf clubs. While the others in the party played bridge, George and Guy played cribbage and talked over their many common interests, including the fate of John Hornby, the man being well-known to both of them.[16]

As it happened, with his 1926 trip, Guy had made his last survey in the Barrens — the department had decided that no further topographical work was to be done there. However, a new plan was developing for Blanchet — one that would fulfill Stefansson's suggestion that he should have a winter in the Arctic to get the real feel of the country.

SIX — WINTER IN THE ARCTIC: 1928–1929

In Halifax, early in the summer of 1928, Guy boarded the *Morso*, a three-masted schooner, its decks piled high with a strangely mixed cargo: lumber, whaleboats, a truck with sled runners replacing front wheels, and two large crates stencilled with the words "Aeroplane, Moth." This was the culmination of months of organization and planning, carried out with as much secrecy as possible. Docked between modern steamships, the wooden ship looked obsolete and had been the object of much curiosity. When it sailed out of the harbour on July 7, the evening paper broke the story: the destination was north and the airplanes were to be used in the search for minerals.[1]

Guy, with his degree in mining engineering, his love of northern exploration and his ability to plan and direct extensive operations, was an obvious choice for this new assignment. The Department of the Interior gave him leave without pay from June 13 until August 13 of the following year, and whatever additional time was necessary provided it did not exceed a year, and marked him down as an officer on outside duty. For his part, Guy was to provide the department, and the Surveyor General, with any useful geographical and geological information gleaned in the course of his work. [2]

The man behind this initiative was Lieutenant Colonel C.D.H. MacAlpine, one of Canada's leading mining magnates, who had graduated as a gold medallist from the University of Toronto in 1907, and with a degree in law from the University of Manitoba.[3] He was a nephew of Sir Sam Hughes, the powerful but misguided minister of militia and defence in the First World War, who had insisted on equipping the Canadian soldiers with the Ross rifle, accurate but with a propensity to jam in the heat of battle.[4]

MacAlpine, the founder and president of Dominion Explorers Ltd., a company whose mandate was the search for new mining properties, had elaborate plans for building a permanent base on the coast of Hudson Bay from which airplanes could carry prospectors and geologists to make a thorough search of the widest possible area. He had chosen Guy to be in charge of setting up and running the operation of the base, at a generous annual salary of $7,500, approximately double his civil service pay. He was also provided with an accident policy of $10,000, and there would be many moments in the coming year when that would be a comforting thought.[5]

In 1928, with abundant capital, MacAlpine had joined with four of Canada's top mining men, Thayer Lindsley[6] and his brother Halsted, Joseph Errington and Major General Donald Hogarth, to set up a publicly traded company. Known as Ventures Ltd., this was a holding company for mining properties in which each had interests and which, by its very name, indicated speculative risk. Already this company was developing Falconbridge Nickel Mines in the Sudbury basin, in an area that Thomas Edison, the famous inventor, had prospected and abandoned years before. Of these men, the geologist, Thayer Lindsley, while not well known outside mining circles, has been described as the greatest mine finder of all time. He was reputed to have the ability to "see into the rock" and to carry in his head a three-dimensional map of the world's major geological formations. As president of Ventures Ltd. he gave lustre and credibility to the stock that quickly boosted sales.[7]

In the buoyant economic climate of the 1920s, prospecting and mining were proceeding at a furious pace in Ontario, as new mines in the Sudbury basin followed the silver strikes at Cobalt from earlier in the century. In the most recent activity around the gold mines of Red Lake in northwestern Ontario, the airplane had come into its own, being used to ferry prospectors and their supplies into the bush. "Doc" Oaks, flier and prospector, had interested the wealthy Winnipeg entrepreneur, James Richardson, in setting up Western Canada Airways for this purpose. Joined by mining promoter, Jack Hammell, they created a new company, Northern

Aerial Minerals Exploration — NAME — with the sole purpose of moving and provisioning prospectors by air. [8]

As the little ship sailed up the coast of Labrador, Captain Randall helped to pass the hours with tales of his years on the *Morso* in the rum-running trade. The first stop was at Wakeham Bay on the Ungava coast to fill the ship's tanks with fresh water. Aware that he would need manpower to help with unloading the ship and, not knowing whether local Natives would be available when they reached their destination, Blanchet was able to engage four Inuit families to travel with them. Two families would return in the fall with the ship while the other two would stay for the year to hunt and help with the adjustment to Arctic life. Soon after coming aboard, they all came down with the flu and Guy successfully used the contents of the ship's medicine chest to treat them.

The newspaper, *The Northern Miner*, announced on August 9 that the *Morso* had won the first heat in the race to "explore the mineral wealth of Hudson Bay." The *Patrick and Michael*, the ship belonging to NAME, was more than a week behind having only just reached the eastern side of Hudson Bay. At the same time, two other mining companies, Cyril Knight and Nippissing Mining, had prospectors in the field using the more conventional method of canoes for exploration. In the same issue of *The Northern Miner*, Hammell, the president of NAME, declared that it was not a race, and that his company welcomed the presence of other prospectors in the vast northern territory — hardly a credible statement.

Dominion Explorers chose for its base a little bay, midway between Rankin Inlet and Eskimo Point (now Arviat), which they named Tavani, an Inuit word meaning "a little way off." During the two weeks the *Morso* anchored off shore and unloaded its cargo, two pilots, B.W. Broatch and Charles Sutton, flew in from Churchill on Fairchild aircraft equipped with pontoons, adding to the two crated Moths brought by ship. Mindful of the shortness of the season and the huge area to be covered, Guy began at once to organize the prospectors and geologists on reconnaissance flights and coastal trips by whale boat.

When the unloading was finished, Guy made a trip in the *Morso* up Chesterfield Inlet to the tiny trading post of Baker Lake to lay

Courtesy of Janet Blanchet

Guy Blanchet and Captain Randall of the Morso *in Halifax, prior to sailing, 1928.*

Courtesy of BC Archives, #1-68462

The Morso *under full sail.*

the groundwork for a base to be established there. While at the trading post at Chesterfield he made contact with Nigvik, the leader of the Inuit group known to winter at Tavani, and arranged with him to hunt caribou for the base camp. They hired two local pilots, Noya and Angoty, for the trip up Chesterfield Inlet, along with a young girl who had been brought up by a missionary and who could interpret for them.

Early in September Colonel MacAlpine flew in to inspect the base at Tavani, and then continued west to Baker Lake, following the Dubawnt River to Lake Athabasca and Fort Smith, before flying south, visiting other company properties on the way to Winnipeg. This flight of nearly 4,000 miles was thought to be the most ambitious air trip made in Canada up to that time. Richard Pearce, editor of *The Northern Miner*, was along as a passenger and wrote a glowing article about the experience in the September 20 edition of the paper. He neglected to mention that the pilot, C.H. "Punch" Dickins had run out of fuel before he got to Fort Smith and had to land on the Slave River. Just as they were wondering what to do next, they heard the chug of a river steamer, and around the bend came the *Northland Echo* pulling two barges loaded with freight. On the deck stood Colonel James Cornwall, the man MacAlpine was hoping to see at Fort Smith, and when asked if he happened to have any aviation gasoline on board he replied, "Several drums, for a fellow named Dickins who plans to make a trip up here next year."[9] The good fortune of that trip may have made Colonel MacAlpine over-confident about Arctic flying. As Guy Blanchet would write many years later, "It is best to begin a new experience with hard lessons."

With the essential work done at Tavani, the *Morso* was ready to leave for the south and Guy "reluctantly swallowed the anchor and accepted life ashore." The main building, forty by twenty feet, served as the mess as well as the sleeping quarters, with a kitchen at one end, a table with benches, and the rest of the room furnished with double-deck cots and a few chairs. Flanking this building were two smaller buildings: an office where Guy had a room to himself, and the wireless house with its masts rising from the flat ground. It was powered for a few hours each day by a generator, which also

Seasonal views of Blanchet's cabin at Tavani, 1928-29.

Courtesy of Richard Blanchet

gave a short period of electric light in the evenings. A warehouse to store all the perishables was set up nearer the sea, as well as a tent to accommodate the crated aircraft and give extra storage space.

On a misty morning in September, two boats sailed into the bay and Guy was delighted to see Nigvik and his Caribou people arriving from Chesterfield Inlet with their dogs. They immediately set up their tents and settled in, like people who had come home. Until he learned some of their language, communication was through the Inuit families from Ungava, or by way of the cook, MacGregor, who could speak the Ungava dialect. As Nigvik looked at the buildings on the base he pointed out the mistake that had been made in situating them in the lee of a low rise to the southeast, where the winter storms coming from the northwest would drive the snow over the hill and create great drifts — something that soon proved to be correct.

Guy was anxious for caribou hunting to begin, and had several talks with Nigvik about it. Nigvik would listen, sometimes seriously,

Courtesy of Richard Blanchet

Nigvik, leader of the Inuit group.

sometimes with amusement, and then go on with whatever he was doing at the time, including helping with the continuing construction. But on the day following a sharp Arctic gale with snow flurries, there was suddenly great activity in the Inuit camp as men, women, children and dogs made ready to leave to meet the caribou, which now would be on the move southward. Fresh meat would be welcome, but caribou skins for clothing were even more essential as winter approached.

With the two pilots, Broatch and Sutton, Guy made a number of reconnaissance flights over the surrounding country during the first month, and saw first-hand the bleakness of the Barren Grounds in the fall with its lack of life and distinguishing features. Feeling that caribou skins were urgently needed, he decided to fly with Broatch north to Chesterfield Inlet — only seventy-five miles — on what should have been an easy day-return flight. After days of cloud, they left in sunshine on September 29 and soon discovered that Tavani was the only bright spot on the coast. In that area, where magnetic interference rendered the compass useless, they had to navigate by following the coastline closely through low cloud and mists. It was a relief to reach Chesterfield. They received a warm welcome at the Hudson's Bay post, but there were no skins to be had, and because of the doubtful weather, they decided to return to Tavani at once. After taking off in semi-brightness, they immediately ran into a wall of fog and Broatch "jammed on the return rudder" and flew back to the post.

In the morning the rising east wind warned them to takeoff as soon as possible. But once again a barrier of fog turned them back to Chesterfield, where they secured the plane with three ropes to a scow in the harbour and settled down to wait out the rising storm. By afternoon, seeing the scow and the plane pitching seriously in the heavy sea, they set out in a canoe to strengthen the moorings, and were almost crushed under the plunging scow. They were blown across the harbour before they made it to shore. In the fierce wind, the plane broke from its mooring and was spotted riding the waves like a gull, heading for what looked like certain destruction on the rocky coast. By a miracle the plane cleared the headland and landed

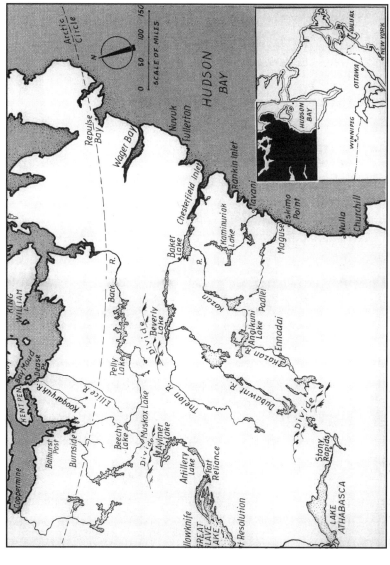

Map 6. Map of Dominion Explorers Field of Operation in the Eastern Arctic, taken from Search in the North, 14, 15.

in a tiny sandy cove, the only one on that rocky shore, with heavy surf breaking over it. The gale was so strong it picked up sacks of coal, tossing them about like leaves, and tore off a section of the trader's wharf loaded with gasoline drums, sending it out to sea.

The storm raged for three days and died away leaving snow on the ground, a heaving sea and masses of low cloud in the sky. The new problem they faced was how to launch the seaplane from the wide stretch of sandy beach left when the storm-driven water receded. Piles of slippery wet kelp had been washed up on shore and they gathered it to make a slippery runway facing directly into great rollers driving in from the sea. Broatch suggested that, if Guy was willing, they could risk taking off from a run along the crest of a wave! Without knowing any better, Guy agreed and Broatch warmed up the engine, watched for an extra big wave, manoeuvred into position and opened the throttle. If they had overrun the wave or slid off, they would have capsized into an icy sea. Miraculously it worked — and soon they were a hundred feet above the grey sullen waves.

The mist around the headland tempted the pilot to climb — even knowing he must not lose sight of the coast. For a few moments they had a clear view of the horizon ahead, Rankin Inlet, Marble Island and beyond. Then, when a fresh wind stirred up an ugly cross swell, they plunged into a grey mass of fog and everything vanished. It was a race against the rapidly moving mists to spot a safe cove in which to land. Broatch just made it neatly into an almost landlocked bay, sheltered from the wild winds.

After their relief at the lucky landing, they climbed the hill above the bay to fix their position, but could recognize nothing. Returning to the plane, they found that the falling tide had trapped them behind a wide stretch of sand in the bay until the next tide, and they prepared to camp in the cabin of the plane. When day broke they prepared to leave, but after an hour of cranking the starter for the engine they could get no response. They drew off the oil, warmed it and put it back. This time with the first crank there was an explosion and a burst of flame enveloped the engine. Quick work with the fire extinguisher saved them from disaster, but by then a snowstorm was driving across the country and flying was impossible even if they could start the engine. They built a wall of stones to shelter the tent, and for three days Broatch, a creative pilot but no mechanic, worked on the engine. They thought about walking overland to Tavani — not more than fifty miles — but knew that at least two sizeable rivers barred the way and would be serious hazards in such weather. On their sixth day a plane flew over but passed without seeing them, despite their smoke signals and their waving of tarpaulins.

At last on their seventh day, the sun broke through, the engine coughed, sputtered, came to life and settled down to a steady purr. While Guy broke camp and loaded their gear aboard under the spinning propeller, Broatch nursed the engine, afraid to let it stop. They took off with a roar, clearing the surrounding hills by a few feet. With the right conditions they landed in Tavani in less than an hour, almost tumbling out of the plane with pleasure at being home. The whole experience had had a nightmare quality, but Guy would experience many more close shaves before his Arctic adventure was over. His rule when facing difficult situations was: "Don't stand on one foot. Do something, for even a slim chance of safety is lost in indecision."

The same storm had also wrecked the *Patrick and Michael,* belonging to NAME, in Baker Lake, and stranded two of their prospectors out in the hills beyond the tiny post. When the plane did not arrive to pick them up, they panicked, set out to walk the forty miles, became lost and got their clothes wet crossing streams. One died of exposure while the other lost both legs to frostbite.

Early in the fall, Guy also learned the fate of his old friend John Hornby whom he had last seen leaving Fort Chipewyan two years before. A party of prospectors, led by Jack Wilson of the Cyril Knight Company, when canoeing down the Thelon River, had seen a cabin among the trees and stopped to visit. Instead of a welcome, they were shocked to find three corpses. Hornby and his two young companions had been dead of starvation for at least a year.[10]

With the arrival of winter storms, operations at the base were curtailed. The two Fairchild planes had been in continuous service without overhaul since their arrival in August, and the pilots were anxious to take them south. Just as they were ready to leave, a wireless message arrived announcing that the southern lakes had frozen early and the pilots would have to wait until the ice was strong enough for skis. This meant a delay of six weeks for the pilots who had been looking forward to being home. It was frustrating for everyone staying in the main building already overcrowded with men who had too little to do. Guy had to use his ingenuity to keep the men busy and raise morale. The pontoons on the planes were replaced with skis, nose hangars were built, and one of the Moths was taken from its packing case and set up. It would be flown by Bill Spence, a surveyor who had been in the Flying Corps during the war, and who had come in with Broatch on a flight from Churchill. He would become Guy's right-hand man.

Guy also organized a seal hunt with one of the Inuit in charge, and established a second fishery on the Ferguson River about fifteen miles from the base. On this second venture he tried an experiment in human nature, sending out two members of the wintering party of opposite temperaments, one who tended to slump into a hibernating condition and the other who was restless and a worrier. A week away in the company of one of the Inuit was good for both of them, and they returned in good spirits with a supply of fish and had shot and cached a number of caribou.

With the cold weather, the skies cleared and the whiteness of the snow offset the short daylight hours. The wind and tide lost the battle with the frost, and ice formed on the sea until there was no open water in sight. The snowdrift predicted by Nigvik had grown to eight-feet high between the office and the mess, and Guy dug a tunnel through it to make a protected walkway, which lasted right through until spring. The aurora could always be seen on clear nights and the pageantry of the night sky dwarfed the base. At last the signal came for the planes to leave and the wintering party of eight men settled into a regular pattern of eating, sleeping and maintenance around the base.

A three-day storm in mid-November ushered in winter with a vengeance, and within a few days Nigvik and his people arrived back, all dressed in new furs, their komatik loaded with caribou. The hunt had been successful. That evening they told of their journey to the caribou plains, the hardships of the early storms, the life of ease and abundance after they met the caribou. It was a tale of feast and famine, effort and ease, inconceivably primitive to those living in relative comfort on the base, and yet they were happy in their success and accepted hardship with courage and cheerfulness. Guy would look back on his association with these people with great pleasure.

While Blanchet referred to these people as "Shoanatomuit," that name does not appear in ethnographic literature. There are five sub-divisions of the Caribou people, and those who were at Tavani seem to be Hauniqtuurmuit, who hunted sea mammals on the coast as well as inland caribou.[11] Because of their connection to the sea, they did not suffer the fate of those in Farley Mowat's book, *People of the Deer*.

Before a day had passed, the area was dotted with igloos, gleams of light shining from their crystal windows, and the sleepy base became animated as people visited from house to house, bobbing in and out of low doorways. Guy visited Nigvik and shared a traditional meal of boiled caribou, washed down with the broth in which it was cooked and followed by semi-frozen marrow sucked from cracked bones as dessert. Nigvik was an *angeco,* or spirit controller, thoughtful and intelligent and the natural leader of the group.

Arrangements were made to have caribou-skin clothing made by the women for all wintering personnel, and when Guy was fully outfitted he set out on his first komatik journey with Nigvik to bring back meat for the dogs from the caches that had been made up the coast. On the trip a storm came up, an igloo was built and they passed the night in comfort while the blizzard passed overhead and the sea ice groaned and creaked below them. The more he travelled with Nigvik and his people, the more Guy was impressed by their judgment and virtues, their ability to create comfortable surroundings out of snow and ice, and to design equipment for the conditions in which it was used.

It was quite usual for the route taken to include a visit to other camps, and on a journey up the coast they arrived at three igloos nestled in a fold of the hills where Guy recognized Noya, one of the pilots they had picked up in Chesterfield Inlet to take the *Morso* to Baker Lake, and Papik, from one of the trading schooners moored

Courtesy of Richard Blanchet

The best Inuit seamstress.

in the harbour. Guy described Noya as someone who "knew something of the world, while Papik was just emerging from the taboo and devil life." The two men travelled together, apart from the other Inuit, and usually built a duplex igloo. Staying in this igloo after months in an all-male environment, Guy enjoyed watching the grace and dexterity of Papik's wife as she cooked and looked after the baby. "Darkness had settled about three and by eight we had

Courtesy of Richard Blanchet

Kaliktee, Blanchet's favourite Inuit child.

wearied of the long evening and prepared for the night, simply and without embarrassment. The seal lamp gave a feeble glow with flickering lights and dancing shadows, the low talk died away and Papik's pipe went out. We lay in a row on the sleeping-bench with our heads towards the entrance. The lamp flickered on for a time and then died away. The thought ran through my mind, 'How natural strange situations really are when you yourself are part of them!' The baby cried and had to be attended to as babies do anywhere."

In another igloo, Guy was entranced by Noya's four-year-old daughter, Kaliktee, dressed in the white fur of the Arctic hare. He left with regret after two nights, and the two families promised to visit Tavani when the days were longer. In the meantime, back at

Tavani, Nigvik with his wife, Shakikna, undertook to teach Guy the language so he could communicate better with them.

As Christmas approached, caribou was needed to make a feast for all the Inuit families on the base. The cache could be reached in two days travel, and Guy set off with Nigvik, Katchooyuk, one of the Caribou people, and Tiarra, from Ungava, in brilliant moonlight. "Slowly dawn broke and brightened. Stars paled in the greying sky, and then a faint brightness in the south warmed until a succession of beautiful pastel tints spread across the sky from violet to yellow to gold. The brightness increased until the sun came sliding over the horizon, moving across it faster than it rose. The world seemed flooded with brightness but the sun was scarcely well up before it began to set following its flat arc. The afterglow faded slowly through the long twilight, passing again through strange colours, deepening until the ultramarine merged into the velvet blackness of the night sky, with the moon again riding high in the south." After a night in an igloo they reached the cache and returned with heavily loaded komatiks through a snowstorm after spending another night in the same igloo.

While Guy was away the men decorated the main building and a feast had been prepared. At noon on Christmas day, all twenty-five of the Inuit arrived in their best clothes to sit at the table loaded with caribou, baked fish, pies, cakes, puddings and jam. They ate until they could eat no more. Outer garments were removed, there was much talk, and when one of Blanchet's men performed a dance with elaborate actions and facial contortions there was laughter all around. The Inuit eventually drifted away to their comfortable igloos, leaving the men to dine on food saved specially for the occasion. Guy produced a poem in the form of a Christmas carol, attached to a bottle of rum, which created a convivial atmosphere.[12] As he went back to his quarters late in the evening, the cluster of little buildings nestled among the moonlit snowdrifts looked like a Christmas card.

This was the third Christmas he had spent away from home with only men for company, although this one was comparatively comfortable. It was a time for introspection, and as he had done on northern survey trips, Guy recorded his thoughts and feelings in his journal. Using their limited wireless connection to the outside world, he had been in touch with a colleague in Ottawa who had passed on the news that Eileen was on a holiday in France. Over fourteen years of marriage during which her husband was away for several months each year, Eileen was self-reliant, and in Ottawa she also had strong connections to both her own family and Guy's. It had been five months since his last letter from her, and he wondered if they had reckoned the cost to their relationship when they made the decision that he should take part in this venture. The high salary had the promise of building a substantial nest egg, and the year that Guy would be away had not seemed much more than they were accustomed to when they had discussed it at home.[13]

Guy worried about being snobbish because he was irritated living among men who constantly used slang and bad grammar, and preferred to retreat to his books, *The Wisdom of Robert Louis Stevenson, The Life of Wordsworth,* a book on Mt. Everest, and his perennial favourites, Omar Khayyam and *The Diaries of Samuel Pepys.*

With barely enough useful work to occupy the wintering party, the arrival of Papik, Noya and their families soon after Christmas was a pleasant distraction, especially the little girl, Kaliktee, who fascinated Guy. Another diversion came when the police patrol carrying the mail called in at Tavani on the way south from Chesterfield. They were en route to Churchill. Guy chose to journey with them as far as Eskimo Point to have a look at that part of the coast, taking Nigvik and another Inuit, with one komatik and nine dogs. The weather was bitterly cold, but encased entirely in caribou-skin clothing, only his face suffered. At the trading post, they loaded up with more caribou skins, and colourful material to trim their trail clothes and relieve the monotony of their white/grey world. They were stormbound in an igloo for three days on the way back.

On another survey trip with Katchooyuk, they spent the night in a colossal igloo belonging to one of Katchooyuk's relatives. With eighteen people crowded on the sleeping benches, Guy was awakened by a commotion in the night and his neighbour informed him, "Baby come." The new mother licked the baby clean according to custom, and life continued as usual.

Early technology — the snowmobile and the airplane.

Courtesy of Richard Blanchet

Earlier in the night, Guy had been outside to observe the stars, using his watch, to fix their geographical position. This was done using tables of star positions calculated at observatories in Washington and London, and printed years ahead in volumes called the *Ephemeris and Nautical Almanac*, with which surveyors could check their position and direction by observing one or more of the many stars listed. When they returned to Tavani, Katchooyuk joked to everyone that they had made a long hard trip only to see the same stars they could see at home.

The "snow-mobile" or converted truck that had been brought on the boat, was tried out on trips to the fishing lake, with enough success that Guy suggested to head office by wireless that tractors might be useful for serious hauling work. It was agreed that two would be sent to Churchill by train and travel north to the base over the sea ice. While Guy waited for word of them, he did some surveying up the coast with Nigvik. As the tractors seemed to be lost somewhere north of Churchill, Colonel MacAlpine was flown in from the south to Churchill, and found them in serious trouble off Seal River, only about twenty miles north of Churchill.

MacAlpine then flew on to Tavani and brought a much needed feeling of life and optimism to the base as he discussed future plans. The winter mail packet, delivered a month earlier, had contained twenty-five letters from Eileen, as well as an offer of a job elsewhere, which, along with the petty frictions of the base, added to Guy's stress at being away for so long. In a private conversation, MacAlpine took the opportunity to express his appreciation for the work Guy was doing, and gave him the needed incentive to finish at least this season before returning home.[14]

MacAlpine's optimism also resulted in Guy buying 500 shares in the Colonel's company, Ventures Ltd., at the special price of $8 a share for employees. On the stock market shares had already risen to $14, and MacAlpine advised him to put it away for five years when it should be worth $100 a share. Writing in his journal, Guy confided that he was going to follow this advice, put half of his year's salary in the stock and forget about it. With Guy living expense free in the North, half of his salary of $7500 was more than enough for Eileen in Ottawa. (It is worth pointing out here that the year was 1929, and the great stock market crash was only a few months ahead. However, it is also worth mentioning that while the stock plummeted with the rest of the market, Ventures Ltd., with the brilliant Thayer Lindsley as its president, went on to develop a mining empire that extended across Canada and around the world from Greenland to Uganda, and from Australia to Nicaragua. Shares in Falconbridge Nickel Mine, the prime source of the company's wealth, dropped from $14.85 to 16 cents, but by 1933, the price had risen to $4, and the company, showing a net profit of over $1,000,000, began paying dividends and never looked back.)[15]

The tractors had still not appeared by the middle of April, and Guy, responsible for proposing their use, felt he must make a trip south to meet them. He set off with Katchooyuk, who would guide him as far as Eskimo Point, the limit of his knowledge, and then find other guides for his travel south from there. Guy's trip by dog team over sea ice was long and difficult, guided by men with whom he had no rapport, and compounded by severe snow blindness. The days were now very bright and a month past the equinox they had daylight almost until midnight. When they finally reached the tractors, Guy could see that it would be impossible for them to travel over the terrain he had just traversed. He decided that the tractors should return to Churchill and he continued there to report the decision to headquarters. A doctor in Churchill treated his snow blindness. He was glad to set out on the return journey by dog team, reaching Tavani on April 28 after a total of six hundred difficult miles.

Blanchet, suffering from snow blindness, on his trek to Churchill, Manitoba, in 1929.

With the arrival of spring, every preparation was made to take advantage of the short prospecting season. The pilots flew back from the south with their ski-equipped Fairchilds, but Broatch wrecked his on landing. Along with the remaining equipment, prospectors were flown out to a wide range of sites; they were to be picked up at a later date. At the base, the aircraft continued to be plagued by mechanical problems, and Guy had a feeling akin to panic as he saw the fine days of summer passing, knowing the field work must end in September.

In August, the *Morso* arrived bringing fruit, vegetables and meat, no longer fresh after the long voyage from the Atlantic coast. The ship continued south to Churchill still carrying the cargo of thousands of gallons of gasoline and dynamite that would be unloaded on the way back from Churchill. The regular wireless reports from the *Morso* ceased as she was approaching the entrance to Churchill harbour in bad weather. After days of silence they heard that a fire, started by careless smoking in the engine room, had spread quickly to the deck. The crew just managed to get away in two lifeboats before the fire reached the gasoline and the dynamite.

This final disaster brought an immediate end to the mineral exploration on Hudson Bay. Arrangements were made by Dominion Explorers for the Hudson's Bay Company to take over the building and supplies, and for the HBC ship to bring out the men and equipment. By mid-September the only people left on the base were Guy, the pilots Bill Spence and Charles Sutton, the aircraft mechanics and a geologist. They were to fly in two planes to Stony Rapids at the east end of Lake Athabasca and were to rendezvous there on September 20 with Colonel MacAlpine and his party, who were flying north to inspect the company's new base at Bathurst Inlet.

It had been over fifteen months since Guy left home to begin his journey in Halifax, and he was looking forward to getting back. Three months of unimagined difficulties would intervene before it could happen.

SEVEN — SEARCH AND RESCUE: 1929

Because of the limited capacity and weight restrictions of the airplanes at the time, and the lack of fuel depots, any lengthy trip into the North first required caching enough fuel along the projected route to sustain the flight to the destination and the return.[1] Thus, before the rendezvous with Colonel MacAlpine could take place, Spence and Sutton, with their mechanics and the geologist on board, set off from Tavani following rivers and lakes, to establish a cache of gasoline at Angikuni Lake, a spot almost halfway to Stony Rapids at the east end of Lake Athabasca. The pilots should have returned the same night, but bad weather set in and Guy was marooned at the now deserted base; even the wireless had been dismantled. After three stormy days, the planes returned having left three men at Angikuni, but with continuing bad weather and engine trouble it was three more days before they could leave Tavani.

At last on September 18, 1929, the weather had improved enough so they could make a start, and despite low clouds and mists they reached the anxious little camp at Angikuni. In the hope of making the rendezvous with MacAlpine on September 20, Guy suggested that they continue on to Stony Rapids immediately. However, with the weight of extra people on board, Sutton had trouble getting off the ground and the low-hanging mists forced them to return to Angikuni. Bright, warm sunshine greeted them the following morning, but there was not a breath of wind to give lift to the planes and once again they could not takeoff. At last, on the day designated for the rendezvous, after dropping all the weight they could spare, they were airborne, and despite problems with navigation they at last reached the base at Stony Rapids.

Two planes were already anchored at the dock, but they were not the Colonel's planes. Before Guy had stepped out on the dock, his old friend, B.W. Broatch, in charge of the base at Stony Rapids, announced that the Colonel's Arctic party was lost and if they did not turn up soon a search would have to be made. Guy had been away for fifteen long and sometimes difficult months and had been satisfied to think that his northern venture was complete. With a sinking feeling he saw his anticipated homeward journey postponed and pictured the Barren Grounds, bleak and storm-swept, with winter closing in as the daylight hours were becoming shorter.

During the summer Colonel MacAlpine had announced his plan to make an inspection tour of Tavani and Baker Lake and then fly across the Barrens to the newly established Dominion Explorers base at the mouth of the Burnside River on Bathurst Inlet. Colonel Jim "Peace River" Cornwall was in charge of this base. Guy had advised MacAlpine to leave no later than August 15, which would give three weeks of good flying weather before the stormy season began. In spite of this, it was not until August 20 that they received word at Tavani that MacAlpine was on his way. However, smoke from forest fires and mechanical problems with the aircraft prevented them from reaching Churchill until August 26. There the two airplanes were secured to the mooring, just in time for the storm that hit the *Morso* as it approached Churchill harbour; one of the planes was swept out to sea and wrecked beyond salvaging.

The fire on the *Morso* had destroyed the fuel supplies for the bases at Tavani and Baker Lake, so while he waited for a replacement airplane, MacAlpine flew from Churchill to Baker Lake, and then on to Tavani. He took Hugh Conn, the district manager of the Hudson's Bay Company, with him to complete the arrangements for the HBC to take over the buildings and transport men and equipment south. Dominion Explorers would now concentrate their efforts on the coastal plains of the Arctic at Bathurst and the mouth of the Coppermine River.

On September 8, the date on which Guy had recommended that the Arctic flight should be completed, Guy received the message that MacAlpine and his group were taking off from Baker Lake in a rising gale, their destination Bathurst Inlet, more than four hundred air miles away. This was the last message received from the MacAlpine expedition. They had now been missing for twelve days in a huge area where airplanes had only begun to venture, and where fuel caches, landmarks and trading posts were few and scattered. It was also the onset of the awkward six-week period when lakes were beginning to freeze, the dangerous in-between time when it was almost too late for pontoons but too early for skis.

Before taking off, MacAlpine had left instructions that in case they were missing no search was to be instituted for ten days. That time had now passed and the big question was, "Where to begin?" General Donald Hogarth, MacAlpine's business associate, flew to Winnipeg to set up an office in the Grain Exchange to coordinate the search, and Western Canada Airways (WCA) alerted their managers at Winnipeg and The Pas. Guy Blanchet was put in charge of organizing and carrying out the search in the North from the base at Stony Rapids.[2]

Guy learned from the wireless at Bathurst Inlet that nothing had been heard or seen of airplanes in the area and, realizing the seriousness of the situation, began putting together a plan. Two Fokkers arrived from WCA flown by Herbert Hollick-Kenyon and Roy Brown, making a total of four large planes and two small ones available for the search.[3] They began making caches of gasoline on two large lakes, Wholdaia and Dubawnt, in a line with Baker Lake, with the intention that two other planes would be able to make the flight to Bathurst, searching the ground on the way. At Wholdaia Lake, Blanchet was on the edge of territory he had mapped in 1926; the Tyrrell brothers had mapped the waterways north to Baker Lake in 1893. The inevitable cloud, mist, rain and general lack of visibility frustrated their efforts for days at a time. When at last they were airborne, Guy, flying in a Fairchild with Bill Spence, partnered with a plane flown by Roy Brown, headed north from Dubawnt Lake until mists and snow flurries barred their way north of the Thelon River. They landed on Beverley Lake at the cache put down by the MacAlpine party, found empty gasoline tins and a ring of tent stones, indicating that MacAlpine, forced down on the short flight from Baker Lake, had camped there and continued on the next day.

After waiting out two days of bad weather at Beverley, the two search planes attempted to fly on to Pelly Lake on the Back River. They were soon blocked by clouds and, with barely enough fuel left to return to Dubawnt Lake, they chose to turn back to Baker Lake, guided by the lakes and the Thelon River. A week of bad weather kept them pinned down at Baker Lake until October 3 when they set out once more with pontoon-equipped planes for Bathurst. As they reached the Back River, a wall of cloud prevented them from going further, so they flew low from Pelly Lake down the river, searching the ground for any sign of life. After flying along both shores, they could see the river was already frozen. There was nothing to indicate that planes had come down in the area, and they returned to Baker Lake.

The problem of fuel compelled Guy to rethink his plan and base the search out of Baker Lake. It was arranged for a sea-going tug to bring a supply of gasoline before freeze-up. At the same time the equipment needed to convert the pontoons of the planes to skis was being rushed by special train to Churchill, to connect with the tug. The rail line to Churchill had been completed only six months before. It was touch and go as the ice-encrusted ship arrived at Baker Lake, unloaded, and got safely away down Chesterfield Inlet to return to Churchill. At the same time, three more Fokkers flew in from Dubawnt Lake, piloted by Hollick-Kenyon, Andy Cruickshank of WCA and J.D. Vance of NAME. With them was Tommy Siers, the maintenance manager for Western Canada Airways, who would become a crucial member of the team.[4]

In the meantime, between September 26 and October 10, Punch Dickins, the most experienced northern pilot of WCA, made three extensive flights touching on Great Bear Lake, the Coppermine River, Coronation Gulf on the Arctic coast and areas of the Thelon River, but saw no trace of the missing party.

At Baker Lake there were now five planes with experienced flyers that could be divided into a support team and a search team. They made one more attempt to reach Bathurst using planes with pontoons, but once again they were foiled by the weather. The wireless operator at Bathurst reported the ice that was forming was broken up by every high wind. The five planes were parked on the frozen beach at Baker Lake while maintenance was done on them and their landing gear was changed over from pontoons to skis. While this was being done and they waited for good flying conditions, a storm swept in from the northwest, the beach was washed out and the outermost plane belonging to NAME was caught by the waves and damaged beyond repair.

At last on October 25, a month since they had left Stony Rapids, the weather broke clear and cold. Although Bathurst was still reporting open water, Guy knew there were enough small lakes in the vicinity to provide safe landings on skis. The four planes took off in formation flying north, and had clear visibility to Beverley Lake where they reached a cloud field. Flying lower and lower between hills and clouds became more and more dangerous. As they flew up through the clouds, contact with Cruikshank was lost. Knowing they could not continue north in those conditions, the three planes found a hole in the cloud over a lake and landed, and the men camped through the long Arctic night.

As the morning dawned clear and cold, they set off once more and were relieved when Cruikshank rejoined them from a nearby lake. Following the rule "Fly when you can and go as far as possible," they flew on past the Ellice River in air so clear that anything moving on the ground would be completely visible. The mountains east of Bathurst, an unexplored geographical feature, appeared on the horizon and they were glad to pass above them and see the Inlet beyond. The rugged coastline and open water gave no possibility of landing, and turning south they passed over the trading post at the mouth of the Hood River. With fuel tanks almost empty, they saw a notch in the hills that marked the mouth of the Burnside River where Colonel Cornwall was in charge of the Dominion Explorers base. People were standing on the ice waving to show that the ice was safe for a landing. Three of the planes landed on the rubbery saltwater ice and, feeling it move beneath them, gunned their motors and sped toward the solid ice close to shore. The fourth plane, flown by Andy Cruikshank, hesitated a moment too long and the plane broke through, leaving it supported on thin ice by its wings.

Fortunately, the water was shallow where the plane went through, and over the next week as the ice thickened, the plane was levered out of the ice, and the ace mechanic, Tommy Siers, worked miracles, taking the engine apart, removing every trace of salt water, and shortening and rebalancing the bent propeller. Meanwhile the three serviceable planes began combing the area around the Ellice River, Kent Peninsula and Bathurst Mountains where it seemed most likely that the MacAlpine expedition might have run out of fuel or crashed. Fuel supply at Burnside was limited and enough had to be retained for the flight south before the real Arctic winter set in.

On the morning of November 5, Guy faced the tough decision of what to do next. Holding to his maxim, "Make up your mind. Don't stand on one foot: do whatever you think best, but do it," the planes were readied for takeoff for a final search of the Cambridge Bay or the Coppermine areas, depending on which was favoured by the weather. Just as they were about to leave, a dog team appeared, dashing full out. The driver, Kingmeak, from the Hood trading post, was waving a message. The wireless at Cambridge Bay was reporting that the lost party had arrived there on November 3, having crossed the Dease Strait from Dease Point on the Kent Peninsula!

The MacAlpine expedition had left Beverley Lake on September 9, had passed over Pelly Lake and, meeting stormy weather, had landed on a small, unnamed lake. With only about two hours' worth of gas in their tanks, they had taken off again following a river (the Ellice) to the coast to help them navigate to Bathurst Inlet. Again, both planes were forced down by the weather and landed near the mouth of the river, close to an abandoned post where they were fortunately discovered by the Inuit. Plans to put all the gasoline into one plane to fly out had to be discarded when they discovered there was almost no fuel left. For the next two months with the help of the Inuit families, the group survived on the emergency rations from the planes and used their ammunition for hunting. Some time during October the Inuit had heard a plane fly over, but their igloos were all but invisible and snow had completely covered the downed planes. At last on November 2, they judged the ice in the strait strong enough to cross to the Hudson's Bay post at Cambridge Bay. In their weakened condition, the group took two days to struggle across ice floes and over hummocks of rough ice, battling against strong winds that threatened to carry the ice floes out of the straits and always in danger of breaking through thin ice.

The search for the missing party was over, but the eight men still had to be brought to the mainland, and flown south. Guy and the three pilots took off for Cambridge Bay but, hampered by mists, they landed at the mouth of the Hood River, closer to their destination and where there was wireless communication with Cambridge Bay. With better weather conditions the following day, they flew to Cape Alexander on the northern tip of the Kent Peninsula, and then low across Dease Strait, keeping an eye on the menacing ice floes beneath them. Guy was anxious to make the return trip to the mainland as soon as possible. At last all eight men were rounded up and distributed among the three planes. Two landed at Burnside, while Bill Spence, piloting the third plane carrying Guy, Colonel MacAlpine and Richard Pearce, the editor of *The Northern Miner*, continued south to Bathurst because of limited accommodation at Burnside.

During the tense days that Guy and the pilots had been flying search missions from Burnside, Colonel Cornwall, who had heard rumours from the Inuit of airplanes travelling over the Ellice River area, had made many trips to visit Native camps in the area to get news of the missing expedition. Cornwall was highly distrustful of airplanes and believed that the best way to produce successful results was by using Natives with dog teams. After the expedition was safely back on the mainland, Cornwall got into a heated argument with Blanchet in MacAlpine's presence about the method used for the search and boasted, "We had you surrounded and would have got your bones eventually." MacAlpine remarked that the Eskimos were still looking for Franklin's bones and the argument ended in laughter.[5]

While they had never actually faced starvation, the members of MacAlpine's party were mentally and physically strained. Some were suffering from scurvy. One had frostbitten feet that required medical attention, and MacAlpine himself had lost fifty pounds. All were eager now to return home before winter closed in, but the pilots, who knew the flying conditions and the state of their engines, would not be hurried. They also refused to risk the flight to Dease Point to rescue the abandoned planes. As transporting the whole group south would require all four planes, there was a delay of a few days until the repairs to Andy Cruikshank's immersed plane were completed.

On November 12, the whole group was assembled at Burnside. Andy's plane made a successful trial flight, and all four planes took off together heading south for the Dominion Explorers' base near Fort Reliance, at the east end of Great Slave Lake. Halfway there, fog forced them down on Muskox Lake, the headwaters of the Back River, where they made a reasonably comfortable camp. A blizzard held them there for a second night, but the morning of November 14 was clear and cold. All hands set to work clearing the wind-packed snow from the planes, heating the oil for the engines and freeing the skis by twisting the tails of the planes. One by one, they took off, all except Bill Spence who could not get airborne. As the others circled he made repeated runs but was checked by drifts of snow. Finally, when his indicator showed the proper speed, Bill turned the nose upward, and the plane rose sluggishly, but the tail caught a drift. The plane dropped and crashed forward. The main engine supports had given way.

The other three planes landed and after a discussion it was decided that repairs could be made. Tommy Siers and another mechanic would stay with Bill to work on the plane and the rest of the group would take advantage of the good flying weather to reach the base near Fort Reliance. One plane would return to Muskox Lake as soon as possible with tools and spare parts, or, if necessary, to fly the three men out.

After the many flights they had made together, Guy was distressed to leave Bill Spence behind with his downed plane and fly south with Roy Brown. However, as a compensation, it was a rare day of perfect visibility and they were treated to the sight of the caribou migration at its height, possibly the first time it had been witnessed from the air, with hundreds of thousands of them moving across their fifty-mile horizon. It took Guy back in his mind to his first exploring trip on the Barrens with Souci Beaulieu when the tide of migrating caribou had swept around them as though they were an island in a sea of moving animals.

As dusk approached they saw the open waters of Great Slave Lake below them and managed to land on the rim where the water was shallow. They landed close to the old Fort Reliance, which Guy knew well from his survey trips, having not been able to find the Dominion Explorers base in the failing light. But they were able to make a comfortable camp among the trees and soon had a fire blazing and caribou steaks cooking. Morning would be time enough to find the base where there were substantial log buildings and a warehouse stocked with food and gasoline.

With the MacAlpine party settled at the base, Guy, Roy Brown and his mechanic, Paul Davis, set off to return to Bill Spence on Muskox Lake, with all the equipment they could gather. They landed at Fort Reliance to pick up a quarter of caribou, but in their haste they forgot to put in a tent, which they did not expect to need, believing they would return the same day. How wrong they would be!

On November 16 they flew north with a clear sky until they reached the upper lakes, when low cloud forced them down to a few hundred feet above the ground. Guy had been over that ground by canoe and on foot, and was able to use the migrating caribou as a guide to Aylmer Lake, knowing they had to cross the divide beyond the north end to reach Muskox Lake. Mist had joined the low clouds making navigation more difficult, and they had to land about ten miles short of their target. When the mist cleared, Roy started his engine to takeoff and discovered the lake was covered with hard drifts that had not been visible under the cloud shadow. As they gathered speed and began to lift, they hit a steep drift at a bad angle. The starboard ski support collapsed, the plane dropped onto one wing, and although Roy cut the engine, it was too late, and ten feet of wing crumpled beyond repair.

The situation was beyond being a comedy of errors and was becoming a nightmare. The missing expedition had been rescued and now two of the rescue planes were disabled and lost on the

Barrens. When they recovered from the shock of the crash, they took stock of the situation. Guy was able to pinpoint their position exactly, finding a cairn from his 1925 survey, and knew that any plane flying to Bill Spence on Muskox Lake would pass directly over them. They had emergency rations and the caribou meat, all the gasoline from their crashed plane, a Coleman stove and a lamp. They had eiderdown bags, but without the tent would have to sleep in the airplane, now tilted at a steep angle.

Having worked out their own survival plans, Guy's next thought was to find Bill Spence and let him know what was causing the delay in rescuing him. They set out for Muskox Lake on hard-packed snow with good walking conditions, following the course of small lakes joined by small streams. As night closed in, the moon rose, but a wind came up bringing clouds and confusing their perception of the land. After eight miles they found themselves on a lake with no outlet, and with no stream to guide them, were afraid they might miss Muskox Lake. After considering their position and realizing they could do nothing to help Bill and would only strain his meagre food resources, they turned back to camp in their tilted plane, expecting that one of the planes from Reliance would be along the next day to rescue all of them.

During flying hours, they took turns standing watch with a flare ready to signal, but days passed and nothing happened. They occupied the time concocting meals from their scanty supply, which gradually dwindled to almost nothing. After the caribou was finished they boiled the bones several times, as they were already doing with the tea leaves. Nights were long and uncomfortable, their cramped bodies constantly sliding in the tilted cockpit and, even worse, the fumes from the gasoline stove began to affect their eyes. They devised a scheme for sleeping, with each man taking a two-hour shift awake, with the job of opening the door to freshen the air just as soon as he noticed pain in his eyes. Guy, as always, had his copy of Omar Khayyam, the eleventh-century Persian whose poem, *The Rubaiyat*, meditates on the mystery and meaning of existence, counselling the reader to make merry while life lasts. They read it aloud, rationing it to make it last.

In Guy's words, "The North teaches patience, not perhaps in little things, but the patience of the Spirit that must meet the moods of Nature through the long seasons and in the surrounding vast wilderness." A northwest wind blew in, driving snow over the hills and building drifts around the plane that later buried it completely. Three clear days of good flying weather followed the storm and still no rescue plane appeared. Avoiding silence, which could lead to too much thinking about their dire circumstances, they reminisced, told all the stories they could remember, and sang. Roy, the pilot, remarked that he expected to meet his daughter — six weeks old when he left — coming home from school when he got back.

A week had passed and the men discussed the question of walking out. It was two hundred miles to Fort Reliance, not an impossible distance, except that they were poorly equipped for such travel. The food situation had become serious and there would be caribou in the woodlands, just a hundred miles away. They built a toboggan using one of the skis from the plane, converted the tarpaulin into a primitive tent, and left on the morning of November 24. The sleigh pulled like a stoneboat and, with two men hauling, they could make no more than two miles an hour. Darkness came at three o'clock and when they made camp they reckoned they had advanced only twelve miles. Guy had always considered walking out to be their last resort and the efforts of one day had shown how difficult it would be. They turned back the following morning and the sight of the wrecked plane was like a homecoming compared to the discomfort of their improvised tent.

The morning following their return to the plane, November 26, looked like a perfect flying day, clear and cold with a red sun breaking through the mist. After breakfast they thought they heard a faint hum, but no one dared to mention it in case it was imagination. The hum grew louder. They rushed out, lit their flare and ran about waving wildly. The plane appeared to be flying on, then suddenly wig-wagged and circled back. It was Andy Cruikshank in the plane that had been rehabilitated from submersion at Burnside. Having seen the crashed plane, he had not expected to find anyone alive and was amazed and delighted when he spotted them running about.

On landing, Andy explained the reason for the delay in reaching them. With only two planes at Reliance, Andy's "crock" and the other with engine trouble, it was reasoned that they should send out for reinforcements. The nearest wireless station was at Fort Resolution and Andy had set off, following the south shore of Great Slave Lake until bad weather forced him north and he eventually landed at the tiny settlement of Yellowknife, on the north shore, where he refuelled. Once again he crossed above the wide, open lake, his plane equipped only with skis, and finally reached Resolution where he arranged for two planes to be sent up from Stony Rapids. His trip had taken three days instead of the one he had expected. More bad weather had followed, and the police began to organize a dog-team search for the two missing parties. It would eventually reach the crash site after they had been rescued.

Andy's plan was to fly on immediately to Muskox Lake to pick up Bill Spence and his party, return for Guy and the other two men, and fly back to Reliance all on the same day, but on warming up for takeoff, his engine gave trouble. The rest of the day was spent making repairs. Fortunately, he had brought abundant supplies of food and they feasted that night.

With his engine repaired, Andy left at first light on November 27 to fly the short distance to Muskox Lake to pick up Bill Spence and his crew, who had been stuck there for thirteen days on very short rations. Tommy Siers had repaired the damaged landing gear with a frying-pan handle, but when they heated the engine, preparing to takeoff when the expected rescue plane failed to appear, they found their fuel supply too low to reach Reliance. They had managed to catch a rabbit, a ptarmigan and a fox to supplement emergency rations that were in the plane, but all were suffering from eye trouble caused by the fumes from burning gasoline in their stove.

With Andy's arrival, they prepared to use both planes to return to pick up Guy and his group on Aylmer Lake, but Spence's plane could not reach full power and the oil line on Andy's burst before they could takeoff. Another night had to be spent in camp making repairs to both planes, while Guy and his men, only a few miles away, waited and wondered what had happened this time. Finally, on the morning of November 28, with all five men packed into Andy's plane, they took off from Muskox Lake, stopped to pick up Guy, his men and equipment, as well as taking an engine cylinder from the wrecked plane. The plane was so crowded that the door was tied shut with a bootlace. If they were to bank suddenly, Guy could picture the door flying open, spilling oil cans, wrenches and people out over the Barrens. This time there were no accidents and they flew into Fort Reliance in triumph.

During the first week of December the whole group reached The Pas and, finally, Winnipeg on their way home. The story had been making headlines in newspapers across the continent, and the reporters who had been waiting for them at Churchill flew down to meet them on their first touchdown at Cranberry Portage in northern Manitoba.[6]

The events of the past three months clearly illustrate the problems associated with Arctic flying in the 1920s: the shortcomings and fragility of the airplanes and the narrow margin of safety under which they operated. Most books dealing with the early years of flight in Canada contain a chapter on the search for the missing MacAlpine expedition. It set a record, still unbroken, for the miles flown and number of planes and pilots involved.

EIGHT — THE THIRTIES: 1930–1939

The news that Colonel MacAlpine and his party were missing in the Arctic made the headlines in late September 1929, and the newspapers reported that a rescue effort had been mounted. But by the time the group of survivors reached The Pas in the first week of December, their story had been replaced by events that affected the whole continent and would reverberate for the decade ahead. The heady optimism that had prompted Dominion Explorers to set up aerial prospecting camps in the North was reflected in the sharp rise in the stock market during the 1920s when stocks quadrupled in value, reaching a peak on September 3, 1929. Attracted by dreams of instant wealth, a flood of new investors borrowed to invest, or bought stocks on margin, with the intent of selling quickly to realize a profit. When the market began to drop, the rush to sell brought the first of the "black" days on October 24, followed by an even blacker day on October 28. By November the market had lost 62% of its value, and the downward trend continued over the next several years. There was a cumulative effect, as people were suddenly impoverished and stopped buying, causing manufacturers to reduce inventory. Financial institutions collapsed when depositors, hearing that the banks were saddled with uncollectible loans and worthless stocks, rushed to withdraw their savings. This gave rise to the Great Depression, the term that is synonymous with "The Thirties."[1]

It was early December 1929 — The Thirties were just over the horizon — when Guy arrived back in Ottawa, glad to be home after nearly two years away. The past three months had been extremely stressful. In the limitless surrounding of the snow-covered Barrens, each person had seemed larger than life, living through a drama at times akin to a nightmare. This magnified the usual adjustment for Guy's return to the city where he was suddenly just an unimportant individual lost in the crowd.

Back at the office in the Department of the Interior, Guy set to work writing a report of the time spent on his outside assignment in the North and adding what he had observed to existing maps. In addition to the departmental report, he also wrote a thirty-one page monograph, *Aerial Mineral Exploration in Northern Canada*, published by the government in 1930. This booklet outlined the scope of the exploration by the four mining companies and the methods used, as well as describing the topography, climate, vegetation and wildlife, and included an appreciative note on the Native Peoples of the area.

Of the four mining companies exploring the broad Hudson Bay area, the two using airplanes had found it an expensive experiment. With airplanes they had been able to cover a much larger range and could more easily see the structure and formation of the land than those using only canoes, but from the air they could spot only the most obvious mineral-bearing rock. As it turned out, the greatest use for the airplane was transporting men and equipment to a likely looking area. For Guy, who had previously covered large swaths of other parts of the North on foot and by canoe, it had been a revelation to view the topography from above. He was able to sketch lakes and waterways, make running notes on the features he was seeing, and add accuracy and detail to existing maps.

At the same time a great deal had been learned about northern flying conditions. Painful personal experience had shown Guy many of the difficulties and hazards that were commonplace for the aircraft of the 1920s in a variety of conditions. Fuel tanks were small and for flights of any but the shortest range, caches of fuel had to be established in advance. There was always the problem of navigation so close to the magnetic north pole where the magnetic compass was useless, and where a solar compass required clear skies. Having to fall back on navigating by landmark, and using incomplete and inaccurate maps, the pilots often found that rivers provided the best guides. However, in spring and fall, misty clouds hang as low as two hundred feet over the region, often trailing curtains that reach right to the ground, so that a pilot already flying perilously close to the ground could suddenly find himself enveloped in thick fog. Winter, even with its short hours of daylight, often provided clear flying days, but then the new hazard came with landing, especially on days without sun to make shadows, when snow camouflaged the boulder-strewn ground or the *sastrugi* — the hard, wave-like drifts — that could strain an undercarriage or throw a plane onto a wing.

In an article for *The Beaver*, "Conquering the Northern Air," written several years later, Guy reviewed the history of northern flying, mentioning the search for the missing MacAlpine expedition and pointing out that although no lives were lost, three of the five planes active in the search were totally wrecked. By the time he wrote the article he knew that of the seven pilots involved, five had since lost their lives in crashes, one of them his great friend and companion, Bill Spence. Northern flying came with a steep price.[2]

Despite the hazards, the groundwork for commercial flying had been laid, and airplanes were carrying people and freight into the North and giving rudimentary airmail service to northern outposts. In the early 1930s, most of the activity was concentrated around the area of Great Bear Lake and northeast to the Coppermine River.

In 1930, Gilbert LaBine had discovered a large deposit of pitchblende, an ore containing uranium. This created a rush of prospectors to the McTavish Arm of Great Bear Lake.[3] At the same time, the Dominion Explorers positioned a team of geologists in the area of the Coppermine Mountains between Great Bear Lake and the mouth of the Coppermine River, where they staked more than a hundred claims on mineral deposits. With all of this prospecting activity going on, the government wanted the area mapped to maintain a semblance of control and order, and with the new possibilities provided by airplanes, some aerial surveying was being done. At the same time the Geological Survey was carrying out work on the ground in an area of Great Bear Lake east of McTavish Bay.

In the summer of 1930, Guy Blanchet received an assignment to survey in the area of the Coppermine River. He has left no diaries of the work or information of the exact area he covered, but oblique references put him in the area between Dease Bay on Great Bear Lake, and the mouth of the Coppermine River.[4] He was at the mouth of the Coppermine when the *Baychimo*,[5] the Hudson's Bay Company supply ship, arrived with his friend Richard Finnie on board. Finnie was the son of Guy's former boss, O.S. Finnie, the director of the special branch of the government administering the Northwest Territories and the Yukon. Although nearly twenty years younger than Guy, they had developed a friendship through their northern connections that would continue for the rest of Guy's life. Finnie, a journalist and filmmaker, was on his fifth voyage to the Eastern Arctic, and was about to make an historic flight to the magnetic north pole with the pilot, Walter Gilbert, a flight on which thousands of photographs were taken for aerial survey purposes.[6]

After Blanchet returned from the Coppermine area, he and Eileen made a trip to Lakefield to visit George and Kay Douglas. In a letter to his brother Lionel, George described paddling on Lake Katchawanooka with Guy using a collapsible canoe, designed by Douglas's father.[7] At the time, Guy told George of being on Dease Bay, and also that he had as his guide one of the Eskimos who had murdered the priest, Father Rouvière, whom Douglas had known in 1911.[8] This was the continuation of a lifelong friendship with George Douglas, begun in 1927 and maintained by correspondence. Douglas was a prodigious letter writer, with a network that included Stefansson, P.G. Downes, Tyrrell, Denny LaNauze of the RCMP, Critchell-Bullock and R.M. Anderson, co-leader with Stefansson of the Canadian Arctic Expedition of 1914–18. In his letters he regularly reported on Guy's latest adventures, usually referring to him as "a remarkable man."

On May 1, 1931, Guy was shocked to receive a letter from the deputy minister of the Department of the Interior, informing him that, because of reduction in the amount of work, his contract would be terminated as of that day.[9] Guy was not the only person affected by this order. A total of 442 civil servants in the same department lost their jobs that day, including O.S. Finnie, who was superannuated along with his administrators, ninety-one surveyors, explorers, naturalists and geologists. The Department was merged with the Department of Mines and Resources under Dr. Charles Camsell.[10] With the stroke of a pen, years of knowledge and expertise in dealing with the North were wiped out.

Guy, forty-seven years old and at the peak of his surveying career, was granted maximum retirement leave with full pay, to be followed by the pension earned in twenty-one years of service. There was the possibility that some time in the future he might be reassigned if he was willing to accept a lower grade in the civil service than his current status. Guy had been in the department long enough to know that he would never be content doing office work, and he accepted the retirement allowance of less than $100 a month.[11] With the contacts he had made during his work with Colonel MacAlpine, he believed that he would find work in the private sector, mapping or exploring for minerals, and during the next twenty-five years such work took him from Labrador to Alaska.

In the summer of 1932, Guy was hired to investigate mining concessions owned by a New York syndicate in Labrador, twenty-five miles east of the Quebec border. The prospector who initiated the search had found gold in northern Ontario, and gold was what he hoped to find in Labrador. Guy and three other men, with two canoes, travelled to Sept Îles by steamer and flew north to the area of the mining concessions. They made the most of their month, using canoes to investigate the area that was a network of headwater streams and bogs. Almost everywhere they saw low-grade iron, but nowhere did they find the gold-bearing formations that they were seeking. With irony Guy noted that five years later, a Native trapper, curious about a strange, heavy rock he had found, carried it out with him and thus the rich iron ore deposit worth billions of dollars was discovered in an area that had been searched by professionals.[12]

Never having been in that part of the country, Guy was interested in the topography, particularly by the sharp rise of the Labrador plateau that attained a height of 5,000 feet only fifty miles inland from the St. Lawrence Valley. In some ways the land was more wild and remote than that he had experienced in the Barrens. On one occasion when all four men were away from the base camp for three days, they returned to find the tent torn apart by bears and their

The goldfield at Beaverlodge Lake, 1935.

Courtesy of Richard Blanchet

supplies scattered, and had to salvage what they could. In contrast to the idea of remoteness, he met a canoe carrying two men, one of whom recognized Guy from his year at the mine near Crow's Nest Pass, twenty-five years before — the man had been a small boy at the time. This gives testimony to the lasting impression that Guy made on those who met him.

In 1935, Guy had another opportunity to go north, this time with George Douglas. Douglas was working for his cousin, James Douglas of United Verde in Arizona, who had underwritten his first trip north in 1911.[13] With the news that gold had been found near the mouth of the Yellowknife River, and at Beaverlodge Lake just east of the apex of Lake Athabasca, and where uranium would later be mined, the North was like a beacon to anyone connected with mining. On a visit to Ottawa he had been shown and allowed to photograph still unpublished maps that were in the process of being drafted from aerial surveys, containing a wealth of information for anyone who knew how to make use of them. George Douglas, knowing that Guy Blanchet was well acquainted with the territory, asked him to be part of a team to go north with him along with René

Hansen, an experienced prospector, and Bobby Jones, a geologist.

As early as possible in the spring, George Douglas shipped several canoes and all his supplies to Fort Chipewyan with the Hudson's Bay Company. When the ice permitted, he and Guy set off in the largest canoe with an outboard motor, towing two smaller canoes behind them, and travelled along the north shore of Lake Athabasca examining the shoreline wherever possible. The other two men were flown in to meet them at Beaverlodge, beyond the most northerly part of the lake. Throughout June and July, Guy and René Hansen worked out of Beaverlodge, while Douglas and Bobby Jones returned to Chipewyan in the large canoe and continued on to Great Slave Lake to explore the country southeast of the Snowdrift River.

Gold had been found in the area, and the shores of Lake Athabasca in the vicinity of Beaverlodge had already been completely staked. The plan was for Hansen and Blanchet to follow the borders of the gold-bearing formation inland in the hope of finding similar rock structures. Before setting out, Guy made a careful study of the aerial photographs to pick out a possible route around the perimeter of the formation. It was difficult territory to examine using the small canoe, with deep lakes set between steep rocky hills. The Geological Survey had several parties working in areas near Tazin Lake, and Guy had the opportunity to fly on an inspection trip with one of the surveyors to observe more of the country.[14]

Early in August, Jones flew to Lake Athabasca to work with Hansen, while a plane flown by Matt Berry picked up Guy on Lake Athabasca, collected George Douglas on Great Slave Lake, and took the two of them to Great Bear Lake. But before they reached their destination, they had other stops to make. To keep costs down, northern planes usually had more than one mission, and in this case they had to search out a lake north of Great Slave Lake to deliver a supply of food and tobacco for Dr. A.W. Jolliffe of the Geological Survey. After enjoying the hospitality of that camp, the next stop was Fort Rae to land another passenger, Jack Stark, a Barren Lands trapper, who would wait there for another plane to fly him out to the trapping grounds with his dogs.

Guy Blanchet and René Hansen in their prospecting camp at Beaverlodge Lake. Blanchet was feeling pessimistic as a result of being out of work for four years.

After spending the night at Fort Rae, Matt Berry with his mechanic, Kelly, flew Guy and George Douglas to Cameron Bay on Great Bear Lake, not far from the LaBine mine at Port Radium. Shortly after they arrived, another plane flown by Punch Dickins, landed, and out stepped Dr. Charles Camsell, the deputy minister of mines — making the occasion a notable gathering of northern explorers and flyers. Dickins was able to give Matt Berry directions for flying to Douglas Bay on Etacho Peninsula, where Douglas had staked out 1450 acres of coal deposits in 1932. The purpose of the visit was to consolidate the staking done previously, and with Blanchet, a professional surveyor, along it would be done with meticulous accuracy. They put in five days of hard labour digging and cutting to make a surveying line through gullies filled with tough willows standing deep in swamp. To quote Douglas, "Matt Berry was a hard worker and a skilful axeman, Kelly put in one day of chaining and digging ... and then passed out of the surveying

George Douglas in the camp at Cameron Bay on Great Bear Lake, 1935.

picture and took it easy in camp. Blanchet, as usual with him, did two men's work."

When George Douglas provisioned for the camp he had counted on the food left in a cache in 1932, but it had been robbed and to make matters worse, there were no ptarmigan or rabbits to be seen. As they finished the last of their beans, they left Etacho Point on a stormy day and one of the engine cylinders began to misfire when they were over the wild waters of the lake. For Guy it was a *déjà vu* of the many tense flights he had experienced when working with Dominion Explorers, and it was a relief to all when they landed safely at the LaBine establishment before continuing on to Fort Rae. The bill for the flights made by Douglas and Blanchet came to $769 — these were 1935 dollars — so flying in the North, in addition to being risky, was not cheap. The bill was paid by the Sudbury Diamond Drilling Company.

The contrast between Douglas and Blanchet was striking. Douglas was well over six feet tall, slight, rangy and fair, with a shock of white hair, while Blanchet was less than five-and-a-half feet tall, compact, wiry, and deeply tanned — almost Native in appearance. When it came to camping, Douglas was a stickler for order and system to the point of fussiness, such as boiling two pails of water to wash a cup and a spoon, while Guy would swish his in the lake and get to his pipe as quickly as possible after a meal. The season of 1935 was the only occasion on which the two men actually worked together, and fortunately their different temperaments did not dampen their friendship.

Things began to look up for Guy in the following year, 1936. That spring Guy received the offer of — not one — but two jobs, both of them in British Columbia. One, as a mining engineer at the lead-zinc mine of the British Columbia Mining and Smelting Company at Kimberley, was in a mountain valley about sixty kilometres west of the Crow's Nest Pass area where Guy had begun his career in 1905. The other, a government appointment with the Department of Mines and Resources as an astronomical assistant at the Dominion Astrophysical Observatory in Victoria, was of more interest to him.[15] While Guy expected that his work at the observatory would be mainly behind a desk doing calculations, the move to Victoria was part of the attraction. Being unemployed in Ottawa had become increasingly depressing, and not only did the Pacific coast appeal, he and Eileen would be near his widowed sister-in-law, Capi, and her family.

The decision to build an observatory in Victoria, chosen for its climate and its atmospheric clarity, was made in 1914 when Frank Oliver was the minister of the Department of the Interior. The first director, Dr. John Plaskett, was a distinguished astronomer who was just finishing his career about the time Guy arrived. It had been Plaskett's decision to equip the observatory with a seventy-two inch reflecting telescope, which at the time of its complete installation in 1918, was the largest in the world. After the first year of use it was found to be more accurate and convenient than expected, and even into the 1930s as other observatories developed, the telescope maintained its prominence as one of the three largest in the world.[16]

A knowledge of astronomy was part of the mental equipment for all surveyors, and Guy had shown additional interest in the subject,

Courtesy of Gwyneth Hoyle

The Dominion Astrophysical Observatory at Victoria.

publishing an article describing his observations of terrestrial magnetism and the aurora in the *Journal of the Royal Astronomical Society of Canada* in 1929.[17] Guy eagerly plunged into the work at the observatory with the competence and precision that had always been part of his character. Some of his work involved spectroscopic measurement of orbiting stars, and within a year of his arrival, the results were published in an article in the observatory's own publication.[18] In that year as well, he was the co-author of a paper presented at the American Association for the Advancement of Science in Denver, Colorado.[19] The following year their article was published in the *Monthly Notices of the Royal Astronomical Society*, which, despite its name, was neither monthly nor contained notices, but was the prestigious British journal which published the results of original research.[20]

Guy and Eileen bought a charming house in the recently developed Oak Bay district only a few streets from the sea. The living room was handsomely furnished with the rich Persian rug that had been a wedding present, and Eileen found drapes to complement its colours. A large, sunny dining room looked out on the back garden, its privacy ensured by an outcropping of rock, and also overlooking that garden was a den where Guy had his desk and his growing collection of northern books. In time, Guy bought a sailboat, *Ptarmigan,* which he kept anchored at a marina only a short distance from Capi's house.

Gradually the Thirties were drawing to a close. Throughout the country these had been difficult years with high unemployment, poverty and hardship for a large percentage of the population. In many ways Guy had been better off than most. With no children, he and Eileen could get by on the government pension he was granted when he was laid off. But like all the unemployed, he had been distressed by the lack of useful work and the feeling that the years when he was physically strong and able were being wasted.

During the period that he was unemployed, and even after he arrived in Victoria he continued to write articles about his years in the North. During the 1930s he published an article on muskox in the *Canadian Geographic,* and four articles in *The Beaver.*[21] Toward the end of some of these articles, Guy quoted the words of an unnamed Native speaking of times past: "We were men in those days." Was this a symptom of the discontent that had begun to invade his own life?

Just when it seemed that Guy was making a significant contribution in his work, and his and Eileen's life was comfortable and settled in Victoria, the following paragraph appeared in the "Notes and Queries" section of the January 1939 issue of the *Journal of the Royal Astronomical Society of Canada*:

> Mr. Guy H. Blanchet, who has been Astronomical Assistant here since July, 1936, resigned his position in July last. We regretted to see him go as he was doing good work and was a congenial colleague.[22]

What had happened to cause this decision? Was it a longing for the free, unstructured life he had led in the North? Was it a feeling that life was passing him by? Was it discontent with too much comfort and security? Or was it just the contemporary term that covers all of those feelings, "mid-life crisis?"

NINE — STRANGE INTERLUDE: 1939–1941

For nearly thirty years Guy's life had followed a pattern of intense work away from home for months at a time, living in temporary quarters or camping, in charge of a group of men, and striving to complete a definite task in order to return home. Home represented comfort and civility, and the letters or journals he wrote for Eileen were full of affection and longing for the day when the work would be completed and he could return to her. Their life was almost a series of honeymoons — long absences followed by joyous reunions. Although returning home meant a return to the Ottawa office to finish the mapping and paperwork of the latest survey job, it was a time for being together, golf games, tea beside a fire, music, a good library and all the amenities Guy dreamed of during months of deprivation. At least twice in those years, in 1926 and 1930, they had sailed to Bermuda for spring holidays in a romantic setting.[1]

Gradually in the new situation in Victoria, working regular hours behind a desk, boredom set in. If there had been children things might have been different. Unaccustomed to living together for long periods of time, husband and wife began to get on each other's nerves. To quote from Guy's diary, written later from the southern hemisphere, "The situation in Victoria slowly got worse as time went on and had reached a breaking point on both sides…"[2] Of this, there is nothing recorded. Both Guy and Eileen are remembered with affection by their few remaining family members, as courteous, friendly and welcoming. Certainly Guy, as he has written in his journals, loathed profanity and outbursts of bad temper. Were there angry scenes and recriminations? Or did their life just lapse into a cold silence?

On February 15,1939, Guy left Victoria on the steamer *Niagara*, heading for New Zealand where he had heard that surveyors were needed to work on the planned developments of the newly elected Labour Government.[3] In his diary he wrote, "Away at last — future in the hands of the gods."

The small ship carried about two hundred passengers, including families of Jewish refugees seeking a haven as far from Nazi Germany as possible. After a week at sea the ship docked in Honolulu, and with some Australian fellow passengers, Guy rented a car to drive over the hills of the island of Oahu to see as much as possible while they were in port. He liked what he saw. During the next five days as the journey continued, he heard stories of the islands of Fiji and decided to take advantage of the opportunity and leave the ship for a month exploring another group of tropical islands. At breakfast one morning with an American nurse who had joined the ship in Hawaii, he mentioned his plan and was surprised when she announced that she would come with him. Guy and the nurse, whom he nicknamed Bili, the word for bamboo, left the ship when it docked for a day at Suva, the capital of Fiji, and when they went to the dock to watch the ship leaving they were amused by the looks of disapproval from the other passengers.

The group of islands known as Fiji were first sighted by Abel Tasman in 1643, but, because of the reputation of the fierce and warlike people who were noted for eating their vanquished enemies, they were not visited by outsiders until the beginning of the nineteenth century. After a period of plunder and exploitation by outsiders, and warring between rival clans, the most powerful chieftain invited the British to rule the islands in 1874. At first the tribes living in the inaccessible mountainous regions rebelled, but gradually they were pacified and won over under the wise administration of the first two colonial governors. The Fijians thus retained more dignity and self-respect than indigenous people elsewhere who had been conquered and subjected to colonial rule.[4]

Guy and Bili set out to explore the main island of Viti Levu and to visit the more traditional villages in the highlands. In the capital city, Suva, much of the commerce was run by the descendents of indentured labourers brought in from India during the nineteenth century to work in sugar cane and cotton fields. After a few days in the capital to get their bearings, he and Bili began a trek inland up a road that soon became a narrow track in the valley of the Rewa River. At the end of a long day, they reached the village of Nairukuruku. There was a moment of embarrassment when they looked for shelter for the night and found there was only one room to be had. The shared room would have to do, because Blanchet, despite his physically active life, was in agony from the pain in his legs after the long, steep climb in the heat of the tropical sun. By sheer willpower he forced himself upright on his legs the following morning and they continued slowly upward through rain forests to the summit, stopping where possible in Native villages before descending to the drier north coast. By using various buses they worked their way back through areas of cane field and Indian towns to their starting point in Suva.

Courtesy of Richard Blanchet

On Fijian food Blanchet commented: "The average meal is vegetable in great quantities. This is said to have been one of the reasons why they were cannibals. I too, after many meals of solid turnipy foods, would eye a plump young native speculatively, thinking of cuts and joints."

After a month in Fiji, Blanchet boarded another ship alone and continued on to New Zealand, regretting the sight of the islands disappearing behind the horizon. The ship docked at Auckland on the North Island on April 4, and he immediately began a search for work. After the easy life aboard ship and the holiday in Fiji, the arrival in a new country brought the basic problems of finding a place to sleep and food. Auckland seemed dull and uninteresting, and the prospects of finding survey work were reputed to be brighter in Wellington, the capital, about five hundred miles south.

Taking the night train south to Wellington on a Wednesday evening, he found a room at the Salvation Army hostel and spent the day looking for possible positions. Finally he met the director of the survey, who recommended he contact the Housing Commission, which might be hiring. An interview with the housing commissioner on Friday gave him hope that work might be available, but before they could offer him a job they would have to contact Ottawa to confirm Blanchet's references, so they could offer him nothing definite until Monday. This put Blanchet into a quandary. His funds were running low and if there was no work available he would have to be back in Auckland by Tuesday morning to board the ship returning to Canada, otherwise he would be stranded in New Zealand for another month. Deciding to hang on in Wellington until Monday, he moved from the Salvation Army hostel to a hotel, which helped to raise his spirits.

On Monday morning when Guy phoned the housing commissioner, there had been no reply from Ottawa to the request for references. Thinking his options had run out, Guy went to the railway station to wait for the night train back to Auckland. Just before train time he made one last call to the housing commissioner and learned that his appointment had gone through — there was a job for him.

Two months after leaving home, Blanchet began work as a surveyor on plans for a housing sub-division in Wellington, New Zealand, which was going through a period of rapid growth. Despite being over fifty years old, with years of experience behind him, he felt like a new boy at school as he searched for working space in a crowded office and scrounged equipment to use. Short of money until his first pay day, he found cheap lodgings, explored the public library and the museum as he tried to ward off feelings of depression until he could be absorbed by work. Hoping to fill his spare hours with some serious writing, one of his first purchases was a typewriter. By September he had had one story accepted by the *Auckland Mirror*, but little response to other attempts.

With time for introspection, Guy suddenly felt cut off from everything familiar and used his journal as his confidant. He wished he could go back and try to rebuild his life, regretting that he had never had a close male friend with whom he could share thoughts and feelings, and he envied the sociable life of the other men around him. From the philosophical books he was reading, he gradually realized that he had been trying to live a dream life side by side with his real life and was constantly being pulled in two directions. The North had been his dream world until it was shattered by the arrival of too many outsiders. He began to understand that deep inside his psyche he hungered for the primitive world of indigenous people — his lost Eden. He realized that he had known his greatest satisfaction on northern trips during his exploration of the Barrens when he was accompanied only by Native guides who still had a strong connection with the land. His brief sojourn in Fiji had reawakened that hunger.

As the Christmas holidays approached he booked passage on the American ship, *Monterey*, for a return to Fiji. He had nearly a month before being due back at work and was determined to make the most of it. On arriving in Suva he was pleased that a few people remembered him. A Fijian on board ship had given him information about a route to the interior of the main island, and as quickly as possible after landing he arranged for a lift by lorry along the coast to Navua. The driver found a teenaged boy named Naza who spoke a little English, and who was willing to travel with him as a guide because the proposed route would take him close to his home village in the mountains for the Christmas holiday.

They started on foot up a track beside the Navua River, but Naza was able to persuade a boy with a dugout canoe to take them

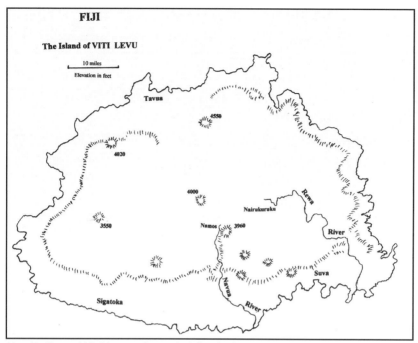

Map 7. Map of Viti Levu, the main island of Fiji, map by Gwyneth Hoyle.

up the river, poling up the rapids, for the first part of the journey. At Namos they joined a well-beaten track through the heavily forested mountain slope, reaching an open hilltop village, nearly 4,000 feet above sea level, late in the afternoon. As Blanchet had found on his previous visit to Fiji, the villagers were immediately hospitable to strangers. In his journal he wrote: "Women usually had their breasts bare when we arrived — then slipped into a dress. Breasts usually immature or sagging — flat — only remember one whose breasts were beautiful."

The British traveller and anthropologist, Ronald Wright, in his book, *On the Islands of Fiji*, describes the dance he had seen on the small island of Rabi: "To begin, the dancers sat — two rows of girls, behind them the boys. They danced by swaying from the hips, with arms outstretched, chanting the music as they did so. Then they rose and performed an intricate ballet, the two lines flowed through each other, broke up and rejoined in changing configurations. It was sinuous, it flowed, and its movements were inspired by waves, wind, by birds in flight and the gliding of fish through the reef. The last dance done by three of the naughtiest girls was a celebration of the body. The grass skirts shook with the hips while their arms waved above their head — the fronds of the skirts parted now and again to show rapid but controlled flexing, quivering thighs...The dance had some erotic connotations but no hint of lewdness."[5]

Guy was soon seated, cross-legged on the ground, and served the traditional ceremonial drink of *kava*, a mildly stimulating, slightly narcotic potion, which is prepared by pounding the roots of a pepper plant, or in some places by having beautiful young girls chew the roots. Blanchet already knew the proper way to accept the *bilo* or coconut shell receptacle, drinking it at one quaff, and turning the cup around as he handed it back. As they relaxed with more *kava*, the *meke* began, traditional Fijian singing and dancing, often telling some great epic story. The dancing, innocent and joyful, could be sensual and combined with the effect of the *kava*, almost intoxicating. After the long day of climbing up through the forest, and the effects of the *kava*, Blanchet was soon asleep on the woven mat on the floor.

The missionaries had forbidden such dancing, and the following day, Blanchet was shocked to see one of the dancers weeping beside a stream with her head covered. She, and the two other girls who had taken part in the dance he had seen, had been punished by having their beautiful hair cropped short.

While he continued exploring more of the highland villages, Blanchet began to wear the *sulu* or native kilt, and found it more comfortable than his conventional clothes. (This harkened back to his year on the shore of Hudson Bay when he adopted Inuit clothing and wondered whether he would ever be able to go back to a shirt and tie again.) He was entertained sometimes by the *buli*, or headman of the district, and sometimes by Catholic priests from France. One night after a long steep climb without water, he and Naza stumbled down a long gradient at dark to reach a stream, and had to camp under the full moon, with only a great boulder for shelter. Guy, stiff, sore and shivering with cold, had only his *sulu* for cover. The next day he joined a party of men hunting wild pig for the Christmas feast, but when he reached their village he had a fever

Courtesy of Richard Blanchet

A teacher and his mother dressed in conventional white.[6]

and had to rest. Later that night he attended the impressive Roman Catholic mass in the grass hut of the *buli* at midnight. The wild pig was wrapped in banana leaves and palm fronds and laid on hot stones covered with earth to cook, but for Blanchet, with a touch of sunstroke, even the thought of food was upsetting.

By now they had reached Naza's home territory. As agreed, he left him to join his family and the local schoolteacher found Guy a strong, good-natured boy to take his place. Their route took them to the Roman Catholic mission at Tavua on the north coast of the island, where the priest served him *kava* and a good lunch on his cool veranda. The talk turned to travel and philosophy, and the priest, questioning Blanchet on his lack of religious faith, hoped that he might someday see the light. That night as they stayed in a large house in a coconut grove, a hurricane hit the coast, terrifying the Native people.

The weather was hot and steamy and, as they made their way around the coast, Blanchet was saddened to see old villages deserted and marked only by coconut palms. After trudging a distance in the heat, an Indian lorry driver gave them a lift to Sigatoka on the south coast, and by New Year's day Blanchet had arrived back at Suva. In his two visits to Fiji he had made a circuit of the main island of Viti Levu and, as he had always found on returning to civilization from his explorations in the Canadian North, he was depressed and would have preferred to be in the Fijian mountain villages.

The holiday over, Blanchet returned to New Zealand and the regular routine of the office and the land survey. In Wellington, one of the surveyors took pity on the lonely Canadian and invited Guy home for a meal. The Dibble family, including children and grandmother, adopted him and took him to their hearts. Women and children were always able to touch Guy's reclusive nature in a way that male colleagues could not. One young daughter, Betty, who was eleven at the time was a particular favourite. Correspondence with Mrs. Dibble, and the grandmother, continued after Guy left New Zealand and many years later in 1963 in a letter, Betty, by then married with children of her own, put her feelings into words:

Men pounding mulberry bark to make tapa cloth.

"One part of me might have been a clever little girl — I don't care for her very much now — the other is really a loner; who liked you because she felt you were too — [a loner] who loved exploring above all."[7]

The Second World War had broken out only a few months after Guy arrived in New Zealand. Although in the Southern Hemisphere he was far from the fighting, Blanchet had a strong reminder of Canada and duty when the ship *Empress of Scotland* docked in Wellington to take on New Zealand troops for service in Egypt. George Douglas's brother Lionel — or "Lion" — was the captain, and he was surprised when Guy came aboard to deliver a letter from George. They had last met when his ship, then the *Empress of Japan*, docked in Victoria in 1937.[8]

When he had first heard that Canada had entered the war, Guy applied to the air force where he felt he had the most to offer, but he was turned down. He then applied to the Survey Corps of the Canadian Army, deducting ten years from his age and, on being accepted, he booked passage to leave New Zealand in July 1940.

Guy spent his last weekend in Wellington in the botanical gardens and then took a train to the pretty coastal town of Paramata. He wanted to avoid saying goodbye to the friends he had made, the Dibble family in particular, who had been so good to him. He thought they might not understand his "dislike of last things—good-byes especially—those emotions of set occasions. It is like a last minute repentance, which always seems contemptible to me — buying something with a cheap fear-ridden state of mind when there would probably be no opportunity to indulge again." The finality of such occasions brought emotions to the surface that were impossible to control. His cool, aloof exterior was a protective shield behind which he hid his feelings. On the other hand, Guy was touched when his friends, including men from the office, gathered at the railway station with gifts for him as he caught the train to Auckland to board his ship for the three-week trip across the Pacific. The men from the office showed some understanding of his introspective nature by giving him the currently popular book of Oriental philosophy, *The Importance of Living*, by Lin Yutang.

With a cabin to himself on the ship, Blanchet had plenty of opportunity for introspection, and recorded his feelings in his journal. "An airplane circled the ship as it left the harbour in Auckland — gave feeling of security and vigilance. A number of passengers on board from the Niagara, — it took two hours to sink, and nine hours before the passengers were picked up…Cross the date line at Suva — island shrouded in mists. British cargo vessel did not conform to regulations and got two shots fired across its bow. Stopped for a day in Suva and met my old friend Stewart who told me about the return from Tahiti on the French boat — no one there knew where they stood." France had capitulated to Germany. Even far from the theatre of war, there was tension in the air.

While Guy enjoyed talking to a few of the passengers, he realized he was not a sociable person. He reflected that strangers at first reveal their least interesting facets and often put on a protective, hostile front, unlike the "savages" who are neither hostile nor effusive, but are always a pleasure to meet. As he did in his early days in New Zealand, he looked back nostalgically to his primitive world among the indigenous people of both Fiji and the North.

As the end of the voyage approached, he dreaded the problems that lay ahead for him in Victoria as the occasional letter from Eileen had pointed out. In Blanchet's diary he clearly enunciated the situation that had caused the rift between himself and his wife: "The worst of women is that they want permanence rather than perfection. My inner life belongs to me, and when I lost those moments, life went flat without them. 'Don't turn me into a husband, I want to be myself and your lover.' "

As they approached Victoria, the colourful atmosphere and languorous air of the tropics gave way to drab greyness, matching Guy's feelings. There were only a few days to experience being at home in their lovely house in Oak Bay before Guy was inducted into the 2nd Survey Regiment of the Royal Canadian Artillery, but those days seem to have brought about something of a reconciliation between husband and wife.

Many questions come to mind. Why would Blanchet, at age fifty-five, choose to enlist for service in the Second World War when he had not even considered serving in the First World War? The possible answer is that at the time of World War I, he was a newly married man of thirty and, as such, would have been exempt from military service. Had he made up his mind to join up because he couldn't face the thought of home life in Victoria and, by the time he realized that reconciliation was possible, was it too late to turn back?

Whatever the reason, by September 4, 1940, Guy was on a stripped down Pullman train of the Canadian Pacific Railway, an acting lance corporal without pay, heading east for basic training at the large military base of Petawawa, Ontario, on the Ottawa River. The train was filled with quiet, serious men of the 1st Survey Regiment returning from embarkation leave and soon to be on their way overseas.[9]

A Survey Corps was maintained as a small Militia unit during peacetime to do topographical work, but the start of the Second World War had revitalized the military work of surveyors. They would be called upon to produce quantities of maps for field operations under battle conditions, assist with intelligence gathering, work with the engineering units on construction of airfields, and many other jobs for which their professional training had fitted them.[10]

During World War I, Canadian officers who had studied engineering at McGill, such as Colonel A.G.L. McNaughton and Harold Hemming, developed scientific methods for locating enemy guns. Using the standard survey method of triangulation, matching flashes from the muzzle of guns with artillery booms recorded on a delicate instrument called an oscillograph, they were able to pinpoint the location of enemy guns to within five yards. This information made it possible for Canadian scouts to destroy enemy gun emplacements before ground troops were sent into battle. The capture of Vimy Ridge by the Canadian troops in April 1917, was a testament to this use of scientific methods, helping them to succeed where the French and British had previously failed.[11]

Blanchet settled into the barrack-room life in Petawawa, with its routine of military drill and physical training. His group was given lectures about triangulation and other theory related to the work expected of the Regimental Survey Corps. In a letter to Eileen he mentioned that they might be going overseas soon, and from what he heard of the nature of the work, it sounded as though they might be sent to the Middle East. The Major interviewed each of the surveyors separately, and Blanchet had a hard time keeping his dates straight and not giving away his true age. He was being considered for officer training, but his preference was to remain a private and make the most of his surveying knowledge. This is similar to T.E. Lawrence who, after his spectacular life as Lawrence of Arabia among the Bedouin tribes during the First World War, chose to join the air force in peacetime as a lowly aircraftsman.

Eileen was considering travelling east to visit Guy, but when he asked permission for her to come he was told emphatically that it would not be possible. One weekend he was allowed a brief one-hour visit from his friend, Richard Finnie, northern journalist and writer. Finnie and his wife, Alyce, were on their way to Lakefield to visit George Douglas, who had suggested they come by way of Petawawa and bring Guy with them. George Douglas, writing to another northern traveller, P.G. Downes,[12] described Finnie's imitation of Guy coming out of his tent in Petawawa so vividly that Douglas was almost hypnotized into thinking it was Blanchet himself.[13] Beyond that, for much of the time Blanchet was restricted to the regular training pattern and confined to camp and not even allowed to write letters.

Despite his love of privacy and his dislike of regimentation in any form, Blanchet conformed strictly to the rules and kept a low profile. Knowing that he had falsified his age on the recruitment form, he aimed to be a model soldier and felt he was becoming a regular old maid about keeping his kit just so. He saw in himself a great change from his time in Fiji and, while his days had many new experiences, they were also filled with a monotonous round of uninspiring duties. Blanchet's greatest fear was that he might not be included in the draft for overseas service, but at last he was given the Canada badges for his uniform and assigned to the sound-ranging wing of the section.

With seven months of training behind them, the unit finally arrived in Halifax in April, 1941, to join a convoy. After ten tense and cold days on the North Atlantic they disembarked at Glasgow and were put on a train to the main Canadian Army camp at Aldershot near Farnham in the south of England. Already in the assigned quarters were casualties from the 1st Survey Corps who had been through the North African campaign and the siege of Tobruk against the Italians. Their woeful stories confirmed Blanchet's growing awareness of the lack of imagination of the officers.

The morning after their arrival, the Medical Officer held a routine parade. Each man was given a thorough checkup, and when Blanchet was found to have a heart murmur, he was rechecked and a note was made of it. After a few days of refresher courses, they were given leave before being assigned to regiments. Blanchet found it hard to understand why the officers did not try to interest the ordinary ranks in what they were doing by giving them explanations. He was assigned outpost duty where he made himself as inconspicuous as possible. On another day, those of the ordinary ranks who had not been assigned duties were sent to dig ditches. The morale in the camp was low, too many petty disagreements, too many trivial fatigue duties, too little interesting work to do and too much regimentation. A soldier must even have permission from the bombardier to go to bed before the tattoo was sounded. At the Quartermaster's store the soldiers returned their four English blankets for a Canadian one, being told that Canadian blankets were only for being buried in.

As a relief from the depressing atmosphere of the barracks, whenever Blanchet had a pass to leave camp he tramped across the Downs of Surrey. His walks took him to the south and east of Aldershot, and he enjoyed exploring the English countryside and some of the pretty and historic villages and towns within range. Farnham was closest to the camp, but long walks were never a problem for Blanchet and he ranged as far afield as Guildford, Dorking, Reigate and Red Hill. His only complaint on these outings was that the English beer was flat.

Sometime during May he had an accident during physical training, and was excused from taking part in it. As he confided to his diary, "Sometimes admit I am getting too old for this life — [he was fifty-seven]. Springs have gone out of my legs, and trouble with feet. Still cover distances, but do get tired and hate to admit it even to myself. Change in mental attitude — impatience with youth and stupidity, and an increasing intolerance." By the end of June, in steady fine weather, the camp morale had improved. The regiment had been on manoeuvres and there was anticipation of action to come. While there was little other than routine to be done in Intelligence, he had time to walk six or eight miles each evening, and was keenly aware of the struggles that were going on in Greece, North Africa, the Balkans and Russia. In July there is a note about an urgent need to organize the Survey Battalion for action, and suddenly the diary ceases.[14]

The next four months are a blank. A letter to Eileen, dated November 8, 1941, tells her he is becoming the oldest inhabitant in the hospital ward in Maidenhead, near Windsor. He is able to go out and enjoy walks beside the Thames, and when the Medical Officer examined him complete with X-rays, he was "surprised to find me the toughest man in the British Army." The Colonel/M.O. was sympathetic, but his honourable discharge was because of the heart condition they had found, and not because of his age. The army had a rule which applied to officers and men alike, discharge was mandatory to avoid unnecessary casualties caused by stress, certain to happen at the battle front. Blanchet asked to be discharged in Britain so he could get involved in the British war effort, but he was informed that was impossible and he was sent back to Canada as soon as there was space on a ship, with recommendations that he avoid strenuous occupations.

With spirits bruised and feeling let down by his body, Guy was back in Vancouver by the middle of December 1941. Within a few months of his return home, and despite the doctor's advice that he should live quietly, he was back in the North and had plunged into a new adventure as strenuous as anything he had done in the past.

TEN — THE CANOL PROJECT: 1942

Guy returned to Victoria, safe and almost sound, arriving home just in time for Christmas. He had made two crossings of the U-boat ridden North Atlantic, had spent six months in war-torn Britain, and received his honourable discharge from the army in Vancouver on the last day of 1941. The rift in his marriage to Eileen, when Guy sailed off to New Zealand in 1939, had healed when he came back to Canada and enlisted in the army. Although his letters and diaries never reach the romantic heights of the early years of their marriage, their tone is friendly and show concern for Eileen's health and welfare. During the time Guy was in England, his youngest sister Helen moved to Victoria to live with Eileen and stayed with them for the rest of their lives. Helen, a nurse, had been at school with Capi, and the three women were support for each other.[1]

On December 7, 1941, the war entered a new phase when the Japanese bombed Pearl Harbor in Hawaii, destroying the U.S. Pacific fleet moored there, and precipitating the entry of the United States into the war. This set in motion a train of events that would have a bearing on the rest of Guy's working life. Vilhjalmur Stefansson, America's most distinguished and well-known northern explorer, had been fuelling this "train" by promoting the opening up of a route through northern Canada to connect Alaska to continental United States, which he considered an essential strategy in the defence of Alaska. Included in his argument was the oil well at Norman Wells, which he believed had the capacity of being developed to provide the fuel needed in the North to get the job done. Stefansson had the ear of Colonel Fredric Delano, the chairman of the National Resources Planning Board, who also happened to be the uncle of the American President, Franklin Delano Roosevelt. Stefansson's lobbying gradually bore fruit. On April 30, 1942, a memorandum was signed instructing the U.S. Army Corps of Engineers to build a pipeline from the Norman Wells oil field through the Mackenzie Mountains to a refinery in Whitehorse in the Yukon, to supply fuel to the American military in the Pacific northwest. From the moment the memorandum was signed, the project gathered speed and became a juggernaut thundering toward unknown territory and unforeseen consequences. Before it was completed, the project involved over 30,000 men and cost more than $100,000,000.[2]

A few weeks after the agreement was signed, Richard Finnie, at home in Ottawa, received a phone call from Stefansson in his New York office with the representatives of the consortium of three

Map 8. Map of the Canol Project, Canadian Geographic, March 1947, 137.

American engineering-construction companies contracted to help the U.S. Army build the pipeline. They offered Finnie the position of Canadian liaison officer and consultant on what had become the Canol Project.[3] Finnie not only took on the job, but later became the official historian and photographer of the project. He continued to work in that capacity for the engineering-construction company Bechtel of California, one of the consortium, on future projects. Like Stefansson, since the outbreak of the war Finnie had been writing newspaper and magazine articles advocating the use of oil from Norman Wells as an emergency source of fuel for Alaska and the Canadian northwest.

Finnie immediately flew to Edmonton to begin work, and his first task was to round up a core of competent Canadians to take part in the job, especially those with a knowledge of the North, an area in which the Americans lacked experience. Finnie immediately thought of his friend Guy Blanchet as the person best qualified to survey a route through the mountains that the pipeline would have to cross. Finnie knew Guy as someone who was extremely competent and, although reserved among strangers, would be sure of his opinions and able to defend them against those whose ideas and methods seemed to be unsound.[4]

Guy had always been proud of his physical strength and conditioning, noted for being able to walk faster and carry more on a portage than younger men working with him. His medical discharge from the Army had dealt a blow to this pride, and he came home to Victoria somewhat shaken by the events in England. While Eileen was glad to have him at home, she had watched him trying to adjust to a quiet life. When the telegram came from Richard Finnie outlining the work and offering Guy the prospect of doing meaningful work in his beloved North, she knew how much happier he would be.

At the beginning of June 1942, Guy flew to Edmonton to meet with Finnie and the representatives of the engineering consortium.[5] In typical "can-do" fashion and without prior knowledge of the terrain, the Americans had decreed that the pipeline should be ready for operation on October 1, 1942 — just four months from the

Courtesy of Richard Blanchet

Guy Blanchet making observations of the land formation from the cockpit of a plane for the Canol pipeline route. Richard Finnie, photograher.

time that Guy Blanchet was hired. Men, machinery and materials began pouring into the North. The troops included many battalions of African Americans from the deep south who responded to the North as if they had landed on the moon. The traditional water route down the Mackenzie River was quickly choked with barges loaded high with supplies. Tiny Native communities, such as Fort Chipewyan and Fort McMurray were swamped with outsiders, as work began simultaneously on building the Alaska Highway as well as more than twenty airstrips and proper airports throughout the North for what was called the Northwest Staging Route, all in conjunction with the Canol pipeline.

Knowing time was ridiculously short, on June 6, Guy flew from Edmonton to Fort McMurray, with Richard Finnie and two Americans, a construction manager and a petroleum engineer. There, the assembling troops were living in a tent city in preparation for the river journey to Norman Wells. The survey party chartered two aircraft to be used for reconnaissance flights over the area proposed for the pipeline. Guy already knew something of the terrain from his

Aerial view of the mountainous terrain between Norman Wells and Whitehorse.

much earlier survey work on the Mackenzie River, and from reading the Geological Survey report of the early work done by Joseph Keele in 1907, but this pipeline initiative would require much more detailed information.[6]

As was his custom, when they landed at Fort Norman, Guy sought out local Dene hunters and consulted them on the routes they used to travel into the Mackenzie Mountains to reach their hunting grounds. They told him they did not like the Keele River, which he had been considering as the most likely route, but they

Courtesy of BC Archives, #1-68469

had a "road" they used in both summer and winter that took them through mountain passes lower than those on the Keele River. Guy persuaded two of the hunters to fly with him north to Norman Wells and then west toward the mountains, picking out the Carcajou River and then following one of its tributaries through a deep canyon. As they flew beyond the canyon the two Dene became disoriented by the speed of the plane over the mountains and were terrified of being lost. Storm clouds appeared on the horizon and the pilot made a quick return to Fort Norman. But in that short flight, Guy had seen that there was no distinctive pattern to the valleys that cut through the mountains and knew that finding a route for the pipeline through the area would be a monumental challenge.

On June 12, the management group made the first-ever flight over the mountains all the way from Norman Wells to Whitehorse, following the Keele River up to the continental divide at Christie Pass, then down the Ross River to Sheldon Lake, and beyond through a wide valley to Whitehorse. From this flight, Guy could see that the passes were relatively low and the valleys wide from Sheldon Lake to Whitehorse, but that the route up the Keele River was full of difficulties, not the least being the fact that it was fifty miles south of the direct line. Fred Maclennan, a trader with a post at Sheldon Lake, told him that the Dene from Fort Good Hope, north of Norman Wells, sometimes reached his post by travelling up the Mountain River. Guy made another aerial reconnaissance and, even though it was fifty miles farther north of the direct route, he felt he could recommend it. He then left it to the U.S. Army to make their own reconnaissance flights, believing that location of the route had now been chosen.

In the days that followed, Guy flew back to Edmonton for discussions and some preliminary map-making, and then back to Sheldon Lake for selecting the exact route from there to Whitehorse. By July 9, Guy was back at Fort McMurray preparing for work on the ground. His diary records his feelings: "Too many men, too much talk...Some queer individuals, many interesting, some pests." He found the Americans friendly and, like them, he called everyone by his first name, but still despised that type of instant camaraderie.

In his previous survey work, Guy had always been in charge of a relatively small, close-knit group, and this time he was only a small cog in a vast machine — albeit a vital one.

Trying to build roads over permafrost and losing equipment in the bogs created by bulldozing away the top layer, among other logistical nightmares, did nothing to deter the Americans from holding to their unrealistic deadline of October 1 for completing the pipeline. The war situation in the Pacific had become more critical as the Japanese invaded and occupied two islands in the Aleutians in June, and in the same month even shelled Vancouver Island and the coast of Oregon from submarines.

The Canol Project was an American Army initiative, begun without seeking the full backing of the governments of either the United States or Canada. The details deliberately were not publicized. The American government began to question the huge amount of money being spent in the Canadian North, and Senator Harry Truman, who would become president before the end of the war, was chairing Senate hearings to find out what was going on. The possibility that further funding would be denied, cast a pall over the whole project, and resulted in the replacement of the army commander in charge of construction.[7]

During the summer Guy was surveying the Whitehorse end of the pipeline in advance of road and pipeline construction and, since his work was well ahead, he flew to Edmonton in late September to prepare maps and reports. There he was shocked when Gordon Turnbull, the chief engineer for the pipeline, told him that the U.S. Army had rejected the route he had chosen up the Mountain River. As far as Blanchet was concerned, the only possible alternative was the route the Dene had shown him from the air, but to be certain that it was practical, Guy knew he had to travel it on the ground with men who knew the route.[8]

There was no time to be lost. The Native people would be leaving for their winter trapping grounds with the first snow. Guy flew again to Fort Norman and found Fred Andrew, who had been travelling that route since he was a baby in a moss bag on his mother's back. He was willing to guide Guy through to Sheldon Lake, and said the trip would take a full month and they would need to live off the country by hunting. Fred Andrew recommended two other men, Edward Blondin and his son, George, both good hunters and each of whom had his own dog team. It was agreed that instead of heading to their traplines, they would leave after the first snowfall, late in October, to help Blanchet and do their bit for the war effort.

Up to now the work had been stressful but not strenuous. The stress came with the low-level flights over the mountains as Guy studied the ground through the cockpit window looking for every indication of suitable terrain for a pipeline. The strenuous part was about to begin. The Americans in charge of the project were reluctant to let Guy leave on his projected winter trip into the mountains, but he insisted that the only way he could recommend the route was by travelling it first. While Guy knew it would be a hard trip, it was also exactly the sort of challenge he enjoyed, travelling into unknown territory with only Natives for company.

It was a happy group that left the Canol Camp on the west side of the Mackenzie River on October 25 and headed across the twenty-mile wide valley toward the mountains. Party leader, Fred Andrew, was the son of the chief of the Hare people who lived around Fort Norman. He had spent his life hunting in the mountains and valleys they were about to enter. Blondin, known as Little Edward, a Sahtú or Bear Lake Dene, was an exceptional dog driver who treated his animals with care and consideration. Frederick Watt, who had met Blondin in the 1930s prospecting on Great Bear Lake, described him as a natural gentleman.[9] In addition to Little Edward's son, George Blondin, they were also accompanied by Joe Zaul with his dog team to help with the early part of the trip when loads were heaviest, and by Paul Wright, who had been on the initial flight over the route and knew the best approaches to the mountains. At their first camp they were joined by RCMP Corporal Ted Balstead who was out on patrol, and swelled the party to seven men and twenty-five dogs.

Thin snow cover at the beginning, making hauling difficult, was followed by a heavy fall of snow that soaked the toboggans and harnesses. The first serious obstacle, the Carcajou River, two miles wide and braided around islands and sandbars, was frozen at the edges but flowing swiftly in the middle. Fred, with his dogs, hauled logs to build a raft and it took many crossings to get the whole group over to the other side with their dogs and gear. A small tributary stream, the Sheep's Nest, or Dodo, had created a box canyon as it cut through the rim of mountains to reach the Carcajou. Guy had seen this obstacle from the air and was leery of locating a pipeline through it. Paul Wright claimed that it was the usual route unless the stream was in full spate, and at those times they would climb to a pass some distance above.

Paul took Guy to investigate this alternative route, which involved a steep climb through thick, stunted spruce. Blanchet took barometer readings at regular intervals to establish the altitudes. After a vigorous climb, Guy reached down into the instrument case slung over his shoulder to make another barometer reading and found the case empty. This was serious. He could not proceed with the journey without it and would have to send someone back to the Canol Camp to get another one. Without much hope, they began backtracking through the deep snow on their snowshoes, when Paul suddenly spotted a tiny hole. They dug carefully and miraculously found the missing instrument.

The two men made an open camp high up among the dwarf trees, and in the clear night Guy enjoyed the sense of remoteness as he looked at the white peaks glistening beyond their campfire. After viewing the possible route ahead, he decided that the box canyon was a better choice. While he surveyed the canyon, the others hunted for sheep among the peaks and pinnacles. The canyon, 200 feet wide, with sculpted vertical walls rising hundreds of feet, had two small streams flowing through it. Guy saw that there was room to build a road either on the floor or on the slopes, and the pipeline could be located there. Meanwhile, the hunters brought in three sheep. Men and dogs alike feasted that night, but it had taken them a week of hard travel to accomplish only thirty-five miles of the 425-mile trek.

At the next stream they found an ice bridge and crossed back into the Carcajou valley, wide and easy to travel until the mountains closed in and forced them to slither along the slippery stones of the boulder bar at the edge of the river. Guy was driving Edward's team when the toboggan slipped sideways and jammed his foot against a boulder. He could not bear to put any weight on it until Fred cut a slab of wood and shaped it to his foot, making a splint that relieved the pain enough for him to travel slowly on snowshoes. Farther up the valley they again had to cross the Carcajou River, and this time the ice bridge held only until the last dogs were crossing and then collapsed into the surging stream, wetting some of the sleeping bags.

In the upper Carcajou valley conditions became worse where hot springs flooded the surface and froze into glare ice, making it difficult to travel and to hunt. With a deadline to keep, and despite his injured foot, Guy kept pressing on until Fred finally complained. "No good, go, go, go all the time. Indians don't travel that way. You don't meet animals along the trail. You must hunt them, and the men and the dogs need a rest." With twenty-five dogs and seven men in the party it was hard to find enough game to feed them all. Guy took the hint, declared a rest day, and suggested that after a day of hunting and repairing equipment, the three extra men were no longer needed on the trail. Their departure eased the load on the hunters and on Edward, the cook, but Guy would miss Ted Balstead, who spoke English, for his company in the evenings when Fred held the group spellbound with his stories in Slavey. That was a language Guy did not understand, so he retreated to his diary and his rough survey notes, always keeping in mind the conditions for pipeline construction.

As they proceeded deeper into the mountains, Fred told them to wait while he scouted the territory ahead to find the route. Becoming tired of waiting, Edward set off down a slope at a lively pace, Guy following slowly, when five wolves appeared and scattered up the mountainside as Edward fired his rifle. Going further, they came upon a wild scene, and found Fred, barricaded behind his sled, axe in hand, his dogs straining at their harnesses, slavering and baying, as fourteen wolves howled and snarled menacingly around them. Guy immediately began shooting without taking aim and the wolves raced away. When he asked Fred why he had not used his rifle on the wolves, his laconic reply was "bad medicine." Fred held to the belief that the spirits of his ancestors sometimes take on the

Winter camp during the exploration of the pipeline route.

form of a wolf and he would never shoot them. Fred's nature was a wonderful mixture of high spirits and Native tradition, and for him the trail was marked with good memories of successful hunts, or sad ones as they came to the spot where his little girl was buried.

The wolves had been following the caribou, and the group hungrily anticipated meeting the annual caribou migration to supply their cooking pot. All they met was one solitary bull, barely enough to feed the dogs. They were about to pass beyond the range of the mountain sheep so Guy and George took over driving the three teams while Fred and Little Edward hunted. The food situation was becoming serious. They had reached the last of the woods and were camped in a clump of spruce, where they prepared kindling to carry with them across the fifty-mile wide treeless plain to the continental divide, which was later given the name, "The Plains of Abraham." Edward returned from the hunt and without comment began to prepare a *rubbaboo*, a stew of all that was left in the larder. The click of snowshoes announced Fred's return, and Guy asked if he had seen any game. There was a long pause before Fred announced that he had killed a moose and a caribou. George reprimanded Guy for his question: "Never ask an Indian what he kill when he come

Courtesy of Richard Blanchet

home. He may have made a long hunt but have killed nothing. He is ashamed. Better to say, 'Here fine *rubbaboo*.' Now eat."

They camped four nights as they crossed the high plateau, 5,000 feet above sea-level where the conditions resembled those of the sub-Arctic barrens. They set out in the mornings at temperatures as low as -60 degrees Fahrenheit, carrying what fuel they could. When they made camp at the end of the day, meat was cut with frost-bitten fingers, but the tent floor, covered with willow branches they carried with them, was quite comfortable. As soon as the fires died, the temperature in the tent was the same as outside. George started the fire in the morning and the others stayed in bed until the frost was driven out of the tent. Edward cooked and they ate their simple breakfast in bed. While the dogs were hitched, Guy emptied the stoves, and for a moment the dying embers would give a spot of brightness to the scene. They would start off in the dark and cold, guided by a valley, by mountains or just by the stars, and it was always a wrench for Guy to leave behind the slight warmth of the dying embers.

The open plain led into the mountain passes of the Continental Divide. When he left on this expedition, the American general in charge of the overall project had requested that they cross the divide by the Christie Pass, but as they approached it Fred advised Guy that it was not favoured by the Dene who preferred Macmillan Pass just a few miles to the north. They found this beautiful pass, almost concealed from view, as they followed a western indentation of the plateau to a break in the mountains between the main branch of the Keele River and the south fork of the Macmillan River. There, the little group of men and dogs crossed into the Yukon, and were at last able to stop among trees and make a comfortable camp with wood to feed their stoves while they took a Sunday off to rest. The deep soft snow, not packed by the wind, made for very heavy going, and again they were running short of food, but this time they knew they were within two days travel of Sheldon Lake. It was a welcome sight to see smoke rising from the chimney of Fred Maclennan's cabin, reached four days ahead of the deadline when the promised pick-up plane was to arrive.

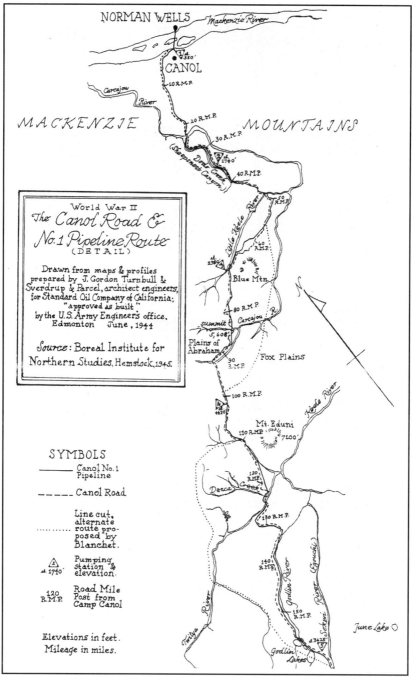

Map 9 & Map 10 (next page). The Canol Road and Pipeline route in detail, drawn by Dr. Patricia Barry, from maps and profiles held by the Circumpolar Institute of Edmonton.

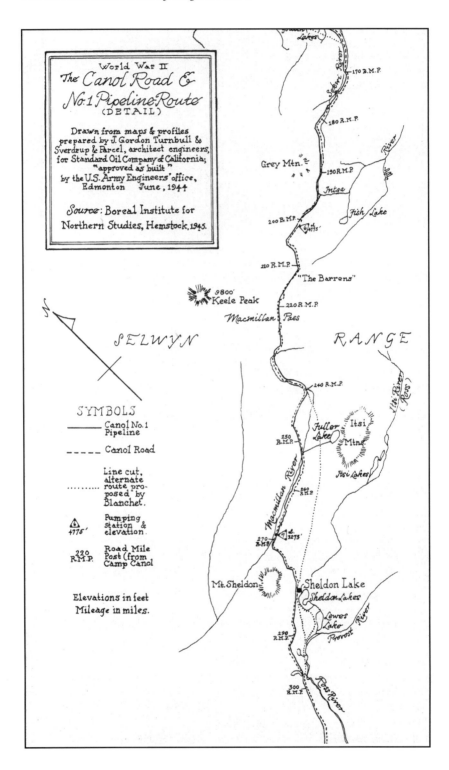

The trip had taken thirty-two days of hard travel, and they had arrived with a few days to spare before the rendezvous date of December 1. Fred Andrew, the guide, bearing the brunt of the responsibility, had seldom complained, and the four men had worked together in good spirits and harmony. For Guy it had been a pleasure to experience the traditional hunting life of the Mountain Dene as they had lived and travelled since time immemorial. It was a memory he would always treasure.

Maclennan gave them a great welcome. He had not seen a solitary soul for two months and was glad to have company and a chance for conversation. In fact he was still talking as Guy fell asleep at dawn after the first night. Sleep, when it came, was deep and satisfying. Guy knew that he could wake without the urgencies of travel, food or time pressing in on him, and his injured foot would have a chance to recover. He also had the satisfaction of knowing that although the route would be difficult, it was entirely practicable and he could recommend it.

After a day of rest at the cabin, Fred Andrew set off to return to the Canol camp on the west side of the Mackenzie River with a copy of Guy's reports. Edward and George Blondin headed southwest to the Ross Post. With Maclennan's help, Guy tramped out a landing area for the plane, expected on December 1. It was a perfect flying day, bright and windless, but no plane appeared — not that day, nor on the succeeding days.

ELEVEN — CANOL CONTINUES: 1943–1944

When Guy proposed to make the exploratory trip through the mountains to find the route for the pipeline, Gordon Turnbull, the American chief engineer, was so concerned about the safety of the undertaking that he promised a plane would pick him up at Sheldon Lake on December 1, even if he had to fly it himself. That day came and went. Bright, windless days followed but not a sound broke the silence, not the sound of wind, not the sound of trees cracking in the frost, not even the wolves howled — nothing.[1]

Days became weeks as they waited. For several months Maclennan had been waiting for a plane to bring in his new trading outfit and the batteries of his radio were dead, so there was no way of making contact with the outside. He and Guy reminisced about their early days in the North when each had travelled by canoe, by horse or on foot. Now, dependent on planes that failed to arrive, they felt cut off and helpless. At first they speculated on the reasons for the plane not appearing, but after they had exhausted the possibilities they ceased talking about it and found small tasks to occupy the time. Maclennan went hunting and checked his trap lines while Guy stayed close to the cabin just in case the plane should arrive.

On one occasion he was alarmed when his companion had not returned by sunset, knowing the accidents that could happen in the bush in the depths of winter. Eventually, Maclennan arrived and admitted sheepishly that he had taken the wrong direction and become lost, practically in his own backyard. Guy had only one book with him, *Tristram Shandy*, the convoluted and whimsical eighteenth-century English novel, with its large cast of colourful and

Courtesy of Janet Blanchet

Blanchet, in Fred Maclennan's cabin, waiting anxiously to be picked up by airplane

comic characters who converse in absurdities, and it provided a surreal contrast to his situation and surroundings.

On Christmas Day they celebrated with a bottle of blueberry wine that Maclennan had made, but neither found it tasty nor exhilarating enough to finish the bottle. At last, on January 15, after more than six weeks of waiting, a faint hum in the distance grew louder. An airplane circled and landed on the tramped-out runway. Because of the short daylight hours and the mountainous terrain to be crossed, the pilot barely gave Guy enough time to collect his gear and say goodbye before he took off on the return flight.

When Guy reached the Canol Camp he learned that Fred Andrew, his guide, had not only got back safely with Blanchet's report on December 10, but had already guided a caterpillar and caboose from Canol to the plateau where construction would begin in the spring. This was the first indication that the route he had chosen and explored had been accepted. Guy was then flown out to Edmonton where there was such turmoil in the crowded office that he never did find out what had caused the delay in picking him up. At construction headquarters all thoughts were focused on the American Senate hearings currently taking place in Washington, which were threatening to shut down the whole project.

It seems that Turnbull, the engineer in charge of the project, remembered that Guy was waiting to be picked up at Sheldon Lake only when he wanted to send him on another reconnaissance mission: that of scouting a route from the lower Mackenzie River across the mountains to the Yukon. This was intended as an alternative pipeline route to be used to transport aviation fuel to the many small airports being developed on the aerial staging route, and also as an added safety feature to the main pipeline.

Late in January 1943, Guy was flown to Aklavik with instructions to survey the LaChute Pass from the air. The LaChute Pass, about twenty miles south of McDougall Pass — the lowest in the Richardson Mountains — is reached by going up the Peel River and following Stony Creek, a small tributary, west toward the mountains. The little plane took off from Fort McPherson and as they flew at a height of 5,000 feet, in good visibility, they could see the pass about 2,000 feet below them. Beyond the pass, wide valleys were flanked by broken mountain ranges. They passed over the abandoned trading post of LaPierre House on the Bell River and radioed ahead to the RCMP to mark out a landing strip at Old Crow when a sudden mist enveloped them. They turned south hoping to reach Whitehorse. The visibility was no better and Guy was acutely aware of the mountainous terrain all around them. With the altimeter reading only 2,000 feet, they turned east again, flying lower and lower until they finally found the LaChute River and just barely cleared the pass still shrouded in mist. As soon as they were over the pass the weather cleared and they landed safely at Fort McPherson.

For one as conscientious as Guy, this method of reconnaissance was unsatisfactory, and he would only recommend a route when he had travelled it on the ground. At Fort McPherson he hired two Louchoux — now known as Gwich'in — guides with their dogs to take him over the pass. He knew that a winter trip through the mountain passes would be arduous but not as hair-raising as flying. In the valley of the LaChute, they encountered deep snow and glacial ice but managed to find a clump of spruce in which to make their first camp. Crossing over to the Yukon side of the pass, the temperature dropped to 60 degrees below zero, but even in such frigid weather the hot springs flooded some areas and created ice surfaces that were glassy and dangerous.

Despite the problems, Guy was satisfied that the route was fairly clear beyond that point and they could turn back. On the return, at the top of the pass, they met gale-force winds head on. The lead

Courtesy of Richard Blanchet

The dog team at Fort McPherson, before setting out to explore LaChute Pass, 1943.

dog, a non-descript little female, was new to the route, but led the way without hesitating. The guide, Joe, was sure that she was going too far south, and continually tried to change the direction they were following. The dog would respond to his order and then quietly swing back to her own course. When they finally reached the shelter of a canyon and could find enough willow twigs to make tea over a fire and thaw out, the guide admitted, "Little dog know better than me. Dog never forget a trail." It was in this area that the Fitzgerald Patrol of the North West Mounted Police lost their lives making the trip from Dawson to Fort McPherson in 1911, and the guide spoke of others who had perished in the same pass. By the time they reached McPherson, Guy had seen that the route was feasible and, from his knowledge of the history of the fur trade, he knew that this was the old ox route used by fur traders and Mounties to reach the Yukon.

During the next few months Guy endured more "white-knuckle" flights over the mountains, guiding pilots over unfamiliar terrain in winter conditions. But these incidents were preferable to the indecision and confusion he found when he returned to headquarters in Edmonton where changes in personnel, conflicting authority and reversal of plans were the order of the day. Dinner with his friends, Richard and Alyce Finnie, or occasionally staying with his nephew Peter, one of Capi's sons, and his wife, were the only bright sparks in the gloom of inactivity and slackness.[2]

In spring, while Guy was in Alaska looking over proposed airfields on the staging route for ferrying aircraft to Russia, he received an urgent message to return to Edmonton. When he arrived, a meeting was set up with people from the various aspects of the project, including Harry Hall of Standard Oil, Gordon Turnbull of Bechtel, and others representing the contractors. To quote directly from an unpublished manuscript, "My work cuts across all of theirs. They give me a flattering reception but the fact is that I have been on the ground and am uncompromising. They would like to get my support and do not like to over-rule me."[3]

The problem behind the meeting was that the American army colonel in charge of operations had been replaced, and Colonel Rogers, the new man, after listening to some advisors, took a flight over the mountains to view the proposed route and saw what looked to him like a much clearer passage using the valley of the Keele River. Guy had already investigated that route and knew that what looked like an "open road" was muskeg and almost impassable in summer, along with many other problems. He had proposed using the Mountain River, and when it was turned down, had made the winter dog-team trip over the route high in the mountains — called the "Indian Road" — through the Sheep's Nest Canyon. Work had been started there, and the spring season was the time that the army should have been moving supplies over the winter roads as far into the mountains as possible before spring breakup. Instead, all the work had been stopped and Colonel Rogers was putting on pressure to change the route.

Guy vented his fury in his diary, "Difficult personal and physical conditions. I am too old to be pliable, and always thought more of the work than of my job. A bit uncompromising and Colonels don't like that...the situation is a bit humiliating — not from any criticism of myself or my work, but in its vague stupidity. I've been tempted to say 'To blazes with it', but can't very well. It has been a drag on my spirits and I question its worth."

Guy went to see Colonel Michener, Colonel Rogers' superior, who arranged that they would go to Canol Camp to talk the matter over with Colonel Rogers. They flew to Norman Wells and crossed over the rough ice of the Mackenzie River by jeep, reaching the camp where they received a very cold reception from the colonel. After arguing late into the night, Rogers finally agreed to stick with the Indian Road. Blanchet knew, however, that the political machinations were as much of a hazard as anything they would encounter on the route: "He [Michener] is solidly behind it but said I must put on an uncompromising front (as though I did anything but). It is the same with all of them, they want me to take a stand and...the blame. It sometimes amuses me the expectation that I can smooth out the rough spots. I suppose it is partly that they know that I am thinking of the job, not myself, and they are mixed up in big and little politics."

When Guy first heard about the change of location of the route, he had wanted to drop out of the project altogether. Turnbull would not hear of it and ordered him to take a holiday, saying: "We have confidence in your route...and don't ever weaken...Rogers hasn't the guts to go against the accepted ideas of where the pipe should go." That night, in April 1943, Guy left for a break at home in Victoria, and wrote, "In spite of the stupid things that keep messing [up the project], I run into friendships and loyalties that mean a great deal...It is curious though that recognition comes more from the army than the contractors. I suppose it is that the army wants to get a job done, while the contractors are more concerned with money. I never know just what my responsibility is, or quite what authority...just now although as a result of the 'council of war' Rogers agreed to go back to the Sheep's Nest Canyon route, I feel that the possibilities of this year have been wrecked by losing the late winter and early spring. I could have saved several millions of wasted money. Due to this vacillating, the morale of the men in the field is low. They always hate to retreat and to face failure."

As summer arrived, the work going west from the Canol Camp had bogged down, but the road building had advanced eastward from Whitehorse toward Sheldon Lake, and the pipeline surveyors were halfway to Macmillan Pass. Because the terrain proved to be impossible for caterpillar tractors, during the spring 110 pack horses were brought in from Fort St. John on the Peace River in northern British Columbia, by way of the newly opened Alaska Highway. Good pasture for the horses could be found only on the alpine meadows, so to supplement their feed, a mountain of oats and hay was assembled at the base camp at Johnson's Crossing.[4]

What had begun as an enterprise to build a pipeline had expanded almost from its inception into three separate projects, linked by the purpose of connecting Alaska to the rest of continental USA. The Alaska Highway was a major part of this initiative. Since one use of the oil from the pipeline was to fuel the aircraft being sent from Alaska to Russia, the building of a number of small airfields throughout the North, called the Northwest Staging Route, was the third part of the program. The highway and the airfields eventually played a significant role in the opening up of the North.

The survey for the pipeline and its accompanying road was organized along the lines of a military operation, work parties and pack trains spread out at suitable distances along the route. With his clear knowledge of the terrain and the locations of the survey parties, Guy guided pilots on flights from which they dropped 100-pound sacks of feed for the horses to the survey crews, almost like bombing raids, only with care not to hit the targets below. Similarly, airplanes dropped bundles of wooden stakes for the survey crews to use as pickets to mark the ground. On one of these flights the door of the airplane fell off as the cargo was pushed out, making it a chillier than usual flight back to base.

During the winter, cabooses had been hauled to strategic locations to house caterpillar crews when the road reached those points. Two men had been brought in by plane to Fish Lake beyond Macmillan Pass while the ice was in, but when the ice cleared it could be seen that the lake was too small to permit a plane to land. On one of his flights, Guy dropped a note to the men telling them to light two fires, fifty feet apart, if they were in trouble, and he would fly over and check on his way back. Sure enough, on the return he could see the two-fire signal was lit and could only observe one man on the ground. A rain storm set in before they reached Whitehorse causing difficulties, but eventually it was arranged to send a pack train to Fish Lake to rescue the two men.

There were four pack trains of surveyors working between Sheldon Lake and Macmillan Pass. In the midst of his work, Guy received a message from Turnbull to return to Whitehorse to meet with some of the construction bosses. From his "Packtrain Reconnaissance" diary, Blanchet wrote: "[Meeting] stormy. Worked out a plan for completing location and survey. Not very well pleased but workable. Too many men involved."

As he waited for the weather to improve so he could return to the survey line, Guy was moved by the magnificence of the mountains. "The scenery is spectacular. The lake changes from green to blue and is set in a deep long trough valley. To the south the Itsi Mountains rise abruptly with glaciers in their upper valley. Massive ranges of the Selwyns are seen to the east and north." The wonders of the natural world always helped to restore his spirits. A few days later, checking on the suitability of a small lake for a pontoon landing, he and the pilot saw a swan sailing down the lake as they taxied toward shore. The day was fine and warm. They took time to locate the swan's nest and saw the hen sitting on it, before taking off without disturbing her.

In the rainy weather of the mountains, the scattered work force moved forward as best it could. Guy visited them by plane, doing what he could to straighten out the confused situation and improve morale. He returned to Sheldon Lake to await the arrival of a pack train, which he was going to use to move further east to have another look at the area around the Godlin Lakes and Twitya River to establish exactly the route that the road and pipeline should follow. He travelled by horse up to Fuller Lake where he picked up a party of five men to work with him on this mission. One of these men was George Blondin, twenty years old, who had been with Guy when he made the winter exploration of the whole route the previous November.

George Blondin, from Great Bear Lake area, had never seen a horse before that summer, and was quite nervous the first time he climbed up into the saddle and took hold of the two "ropes" to steer it. Later he amused the group by asking, "What do horses do when they play?" Guy had not been in a saddle since his days of managing the coal mine in the Crow's Nest Pass area in 1906, but he adjusted quickly and became quite attached to Jennifer, his little black mare.

The little group left the main party and travelled ahead, up over Macmillan Pass and down across the wide plateau of rolling country. To Guy, the rolling hills were green and welcoming, and he enjoyed the contrast with the bleak winter scene he had experienced on that same plateau in November of the previous year. They followed a saddle between two mountains, trying to pick a route that avoided the streams coming from the springs on the hillsides. After several moose sightings, George Blondin was dispatched to hunt. George missed his first shot, and went off to follow the moose. After they had waited for more than an hour, Guy left two of the packers behind to wait for George and continued on to make camp near the

Intga River. Rain kept them in camp all day and still the hunters did not reappear, so another man was sent to find them. After two days all the men finally reappeared, having lost the trail several times and having to backtrack through swampy ground.

As the little party continued they met another large group of surveyors who had arrived at their location without tents, axes, anything to cook with, and indeed, without any food — something that could never have happened on Guy's early surveys. Fortunately, a plane arrived from Canol Camp with their supplies and reported that things were at last progressing better at that end of the pipeline. Guy took the opportunity for a flight over the terrain that lay ahead, and to make contact with the five different parties spread out at various places along the western part of the route. When he was satisfied that all was going well, he set off again with George Blondin, three others and eleven horses, glad to be away from "the mob," and on horseback once more. It was interesting to him to find their old camping places from the original winter trip.

Their route lay between the Godlin Lakes and along the Godlin River. At one of their camping spots a grizzly bear climbed a large tree nearby and perched there for the night. When they broke camp early in the morning, they disturbed the bear, which fled up the mountain. The river here flowed through a well-defined valley, full of stones and rocks that were hard on the horses feet. The horses' hooves became so badly worn that their shoes started dropping off. On this rough ground, Jennifer, would stop and look around at him as if to say, "Aren't you going to get off?," and Blanchet would usually oblige.

Approaching the valley between the Godlin River and the Twitya River (which Guy always called the Tooritchie), Guy, as always, was searching for the best way through. He tried out both slopes and the bottom, finding all were bad, hard on the horses and dangerous in spots. He noted that while a wide valley with moderate slopes looks like the right location, the drainage on such slopes is slow and forms underground springs, making for a bad surface and with little material for building the road that would accompany the pipeline. They climbed a hog's back separating the two valleys and held to the upper slopes.

Satisfied with their progress, they camped on a sandbar of the Tooritchie and contemplated crossing it the next day. Seven miles before its confluence with the Keele River, the river is fast moving, 200 feet wide, and deep enough to require swimming or rafting. Most of the horses could swim across with their packs, but the horses that Guy and George Blondin were riding had short legs and with riders on them would be swept away by the current. George recounted the story of his involvement in the Canol Project much later in his life, after he had become a published author, and it is included as an appendix to a history of the project. In his words, "Blanchet was an old man and probably could drown." Guy, even though he was forty years older than George, still prided himself on his physical condition and his ability to keep up with, or outwork, younger men, and would not have appreciated that comment.[5]

Guy and George Blondin searched for wood to make a raft and finding only a couple of big pieces, roped them together to form a crosspiece and piled small wood underneath it. They towed their makeshift craft upstream to the narrowest part of the river and, with another man from the group designated to catch their rope on the other side, pushed off into the current. They were unable to control the raft with their pole and the current swept them past the man who was to bring them ashore. The current pulled the raft out into deep water and they found themselves rushing towards rapids and cliffs. The man waded out as far as he dared and they threw him a rope. He missed the catch but scrambled to grab it at the water's edge, braced himself against a rock and gradually stopped the raft in its race downstream. As the man reeled them in, he pulled too hard and the raft began to sink. George remembered that he was holding the rope with one hand and Guy's belt with the other, as the water closed over Guy's head.

Guy's great concern was not for his life but for his briefcase that held his papers — if he lost it the whole trip would have been wasted. Such a concern was beyond George Blondin's understanding — saving their lives was all that mattered to him. When they reached the shore, however, the briefcase had survived. They made camp even though it was only the middle of the day, built a fire and Guy spent the rest of the day drying out his precious papers. In the words of George, "We was kind of mad at each other, and we're all wet."

The next day Blanchet and his men moved on and reached a fan of glacial material on Devil Creek. George Blondin went up the nearest mountain to hunt sheep, and found a large camp of Mountain Dene with their pack dogs. George had somehow known by moccasin telegraph that he would meet people that day, a feature of aboriginal life that fascinated Guy. It was a pleasure for Guy to meet the five or six families, including babies and grandmothers, and to see how they lived off the country, wandering through the mountains in summer and ending their journeys at the upper waters of the rivers. That area was moose country and, after killing all the moose they needed and drying the meat, they built large boats out of the untanned skins, loaded them with people and dogs, and made a swift descent down wild rivers to the Mackenzie. (These boats were up to forty feet long and could carry two tons of cargo. Because they would be dismantled when they reached the Mackenzie, and the skins used for other purposes, no original examples remain, although the Prince of Wales Northern Heritage Centre in Yellowknife has one on exhibit, which was constructed there.)

Guy and his men were now only fifteen or twenty miles away from the survey crews working out from the Canol Camp. George Blondin, feeling the pull of home, announced that he would like to quit and make for Norman Wells on foot. Guy was agreeable, gave him an eiderdown, and watched him go, full of "Indian self-assurance." In Guy's words, "He is a good boy for a trip, capable and willing." He had hoped to meet the crews from Canol Camp but they were taking longer than expected, so Guy and his men turned back to explore an alternative route west of the one by which they had come, as always, looking for a better way. On a fine summer evening they camped near the summit of Deka Pass, and Guy enjoyed the views back to the rugged mountains between the Twitya and Carcajou rivers where they had just been. Their horses disturbed a large band of sheep that fled up the mountain, and a flock of ptarmigan provided their evening meal. While this route was higher, the footings and food for the horses were better, and though the gradients were steep it seemed to be a better route for the pipeline. They reached the Twitya River higher up than the previous crossing where he had nearly drowned and, although it was wide and swift, they were able to ford it.

It was now the beginning of September and snow had fallen far down the sides of the mountains. Finding their way blocked by a mudslide on one side of a valley and a rock slide on the other, they had to work their way back to the river and try again. For a time Guy could not see a way out of the valley, but, using his skill as a topographer, all gradually became clear and they arrived back at the base camp where they had started twelve days previously. The return route had been longer, but it satisfied his need to make improvements.

There were several survey crews working between the base camp and Sheldon Lake, and Guy immediately began to hear about various problems that some of them were having. Blanchet supplied food from his cache to a surveyor who had lost everything when he had been tipped off his horse into the Godlin River, escaping serious injury when the horse fell on him. Next he heard the work was going slowly up the track toward Sheldon Lake and went back to investigate. He soon met another survey party advancing despite heavy snowstorms and problems with grizzly bears. Finally, all going well, he made for the lake where he had started his reconnaissance, and where he would be picked up by plane. With the airplane they flew along the pipeline route continuing to drop horse feed and other supplies to the men.

Guy described getting back to Sheldon Lake: "Met S. — who said he was in charge and asked where I had been! I was a bit travel worn and this question from this man was too much. I said, 'As far as I know you don't even exist.' " This vignette captures perfectly Blanchet's frustrations with the organization of the project. Travel worn is a serious understatement for a man who had made three difficult trips, two of them in winter, and who had been living out of a suitcase or a pack for more than a year. Even when he was in Edmonton, often the only space for him to sleep was in an attic room used by travelling salesmen to display their wares. Things were no better in the engineering office where he had no desk of his own and would be given the corner of a table to write his reports. Only the office of the secretaries, staffed by girls from the south, provided a bright spot in the Edmonton offices.

After the flight back from Sheldon Lake, Guy's involvement with the Canol Pipeline came to an end. Back in Edmonton, Gordon Turnbull presented him with a watch, thanked him for the work he had done, and asked him to take one last look over the pipeline. "This proved to be more or less of a joy ride...plane to Norman Wells, station waggon with driver from there, camps along the way for meals and sleep."[6]

One of his survey colleagues wrote a long saga in doggerel, which was read at the party to mark the completion of the work, including these verses:

> They got an explorer by name of Blanchet
> Absolutely the toughest Canadian yet
> He would out-walk a Cree over muskeg and logs
> And once up the Tanana, outwalked the dogs.
>
> So they started him out about the 1st of November
> I'll bet a new hat that's a day he'll remember
> When winter starts off in the Arctic, old Topper
> There ain't a damn thing you can do that will stop her.
>
> So Guy with his guides and his huskies and sleds
> Hit off down the trail with their eiderdown beds
> "Godamit," says Turnbull, "Be sure to remember
> We'll meet at the Lake the first of December."[7]

The "golden" weld that joined the two sections of pipeline occurred in February, 1944, at Macmillan Pass, and by April oil was flowing through to the refinery at Whitehorse. But the emergency that had prompted the project in the first place no longer existed, and within six months it was abandoned and the hard-won road and pipeline gradually became once more the domain of the grizzly bears, moose and mountain sheep. It is now officially designated as a hiking trail and the machines that litter it are returning to nature as part of the scenery.

Years later, long after the pipeline had been abandoned and become a hiking trail, S.R. Gage in his book, *A Walk on the Canol Road*, described crossing the Twitya River where Guy had nearly come to grief when his raft sank. When Gage reached the river, he found four oil drums lashed into a frame of driftwood in a somewhat dilapidated state of repair. He spent time refurbishing the raft, and then tried to drag it upstream to a narrower part of the river. It was late in the afternoon when he was ready to attempt the crossing, stripped down to his underwear, his pack secured inside plastic bags, and with a couple of rough-hewn paddles and a pole to use. When he hit the main section of the river, the current grabbed the raft and moved him out into the centre where it quickly became too deep for the pole to reach bottom. In his own words, "The idea of one man paddling four oil drums against the Twitya proved to be a very bad joke. I was facing upstream…and watching the shore whiz by over my shoulder. The current had me in its grip. I might as well have been paddling with a soup spoon or a spatula." He tried a draw stroke to move the raft sideways. Knowing of the rapids downstream as well as the cliffs, he resigned himself "to paddling until my arms gave out or I had a heart attack." The draw stroke had moved the raft into a ferry position, well-known to canoeists, and with the shore line hurtling by, the current gradually brought him close enough to shore to jump off and pull the raft in, leaving him relieved but emotionally and physically drained. A previous group had used a swimmer in a wetsuit to take a rope across to the other side, but even they had run into great difficulties. This quotation gives a picture of some of the difficult and dangerous conditions Guy had experienced.[8]

Guy summed up his feelings in his diary. "At the inception nobody took the trouble to make the most elementary calculations of materials to be transported and existing transportation. There was too much stress on machines to move dirt. Surface swamp and permafrost were problems that were ignored until each new man in control learned by experience what he could have been told at the start. There were times when a few men with picks and shovels would have saved the day, but there were none. Incredible difficulties and hardships were met by the field men, while the vast office staff stayed behind at their desks."[9]

Patton, the man in charge of the survey, knew nothing of the country, and while Guy liked him personally he felt that Patton was intruding on northern territory where Guy had begun surveying in the 1920s. There was only one man in the organization with whom he felt real rapport, Harry Hall, the engineer from Standard Oil, and this was a connection that would prove valuable in the future.

TWELVE — FINAL WORKING YEARS: 1944–1954

The Depression ended in Canada with the Second World War. War-time construction projects in the North such as the Canol Pipeline, the Alaska Highway and the Northwest Staging Route, all brought new interest surging into a region that had long been overlooked. The Department of Mines and Resources had replaced the Department of the Interior and was ready once more to send surveyors into the field.

While Guy was still working on the Canol Project, in February of 1944, he received a telegram sent to him in care of Gordon Turnbull's office in Edmonton from F.H. Peters, the surveyor-general of Canada, offering him a position in charge of a base line survey somewhere in the North. In his reply to Mr. Peters, he explained that he had not yet been released from the Canol Project but, knowing that the completion of the pipeline was imminent, he thought that he might be available and requested more information about the location and the urgency of the job.

While completing his final work on the Canol project, Guy applied to work on a new pipeline that was being proposed for Saudi Arabia. Feeling it might be the last big job he would be able to tackle, he was more drawn to the one that would give him new experiences in an entirely foreign area, in preference to work in the familiar Mackenzie River district. With the contacts he had made in the oil industry, and being the only senior Canadian working on Canol, he thought his application to work in Arabia might have some advantage over others.

By March 1944, however, Guy learned that the Arabian job had been put on hold, so he accepted the offer from the surveyor-general to do the base-line survey for the Canadian department. The job was to extend the 6th meridian from the point at which it had stopped in 1922, going as far north as the season would permit. The purpose was to facilitate the accurate surveying of mining and oil field claims in the area between Great Slave Lake and Great Bear Lake.[1]

This was routine work for Guy and he has left no record of it. On the other hand, it was a novelty to three teenagers from Edmonton, hired by Blanchet as assistants. In 1944, most able-bodied men were either in the armed forces or employed in essential work in factories or farms across the country. High school students found jobs working for American Army projects, both in the summer and part-time during the school year, and had become accustomed to earning a lot of money in relatively easy conditions. Even the men from Native communities in the North had been affected by the proximity of American bases and work opportunities. In Edmonton, where previously Guy would have had a wide choice of experienced men, the labour pool was limited and he hired three sixteen- or seventeen-year-olds, just out of Grade 11 in high school and eager to go north in search of adventure.

Starting from Edmonton on June 13, Guy and the boys enjoyed the trip north on the rough railway line to Waterways, a route Blanchet had travelled many times during his early survey work in the North. The bunks in the sleeping cars were equipped with safety nets to catch those who were tossed out of bed when the train lurched. Next, they travelled down the Athabasca River to Fitzgerald on a Hudson's Bay Company sternwheeler, pushing freight barges ahead of it, and crossed the eighteen-mile portage to Fort Smith in the Northwest Territories in a taxi. In Fort Smith they had to wait a few days for the next boat, *Distributor,* to take them to the beginning of the Mackenzie River where the work would begin. Guy made use of the break to give the boys some practice in basic survey technique, teaching them to drop a plumb bob, mark the spot, measure the angle of slope, and stretch the steel tape and surveyor's chain straight to make accurate measurements. This involved cutting down all bushes and trees standing in the way of the line, followed by much walking back and forth before they could move on to the next spot.

On July 3 they reached Fort Providence, at the west end of Great Slave Lake, where the Mackenzie River begins, loaded all their gear onto a motorized barge belonging to the survey, and headed down the Mackenzie River into Mills Lake. There they set up the base camp. Apart from the days of practice surveying, the boys had found the three-week journey more like a holiday adventure than work. Altogether Guy had recruited a survey crew of eight, along with a dozen Dene from Fort Providence to work as axemen, clearing trees and brush from the line. Their starting point, the place where the 1922 survey ended, was at least thirty miles due south, and the first order of business was to move equipment and enough supplies to last until their new survey line reached the base camp.

The base camp was close to an American emergency landing strip where piles of abandoned equipment were waiting to be shipped south. Guy searched among the machinery, found a bulldozer, attached a sleigh to it and loaded on their equipment and supplies, hoping they could drive it south to the starting point and avoid a thirty-mile portage. The ground was muskeg, lying over permafrost, and the Native men were sent ahead to build bridges over any creeks to be crossed. At the first bridge the bulldozer broke through and went into the creek. Guy walked back to the base camp, found a caterpillar tractor, drove it back and winched the bulldozer out of the creek. At the next bridge both machines broke through and sank into the muskeg! Now there was no alternative but to portage, and all set off with seventy-five-pound packs on their backs.

At last, on July 11, after a week of struggling through muskeg, in rainstorms followed by heat and drought, beset by ravenous blackflies and mosquitoes, they found the starting point of the survey. The plan was to survey back to the Mackenzie River by the first week of August, cross to the opposite bank and continue north as far as they could go in the season.

After two days, three of the Native axemen quit and left for home. Guy left the transit man in charge of the party and walked back to Fort Providence to recruit more men. Despite working through burned-over areas full of fallen trees, and close calls from the lightning during thunderstorms, the work done by the boys from Edmonton began to improve and they were getting stronger. More axemen quit and went home to the Mackenzie River, and Guy walked out to Fort Providence a second time bringing back the unwilling workers and some additional ones, along with the mail — the first mail the boys from Edmonton had received since they left home.

Rain, sleet and snow gave way to a heat wave so fierce in mid-July that work was switched to nighttime and they slept during the day. By the end of the first hot week, Guy gave the crew a day off to walk out to the river — much closer now — to have a bath and get a change of clothes from the barge at their base. By July 29, they were only three-and-a-half miles from the Mackenzie River. The job was going well, but the boys hated the working conditions: the lack of water, temperatures over 100 degrees Fahrenheit, bugs and the steady diet of beans, bacon and bannock.

For the three teenagers from Edmonton, this had been the toughest work they had ever done. To quote an article, "Summer Job Adventures for a Young Edmonton Student in 1943 and 1944" written many years later by Les Faulkner, and published in *Three Northern Wartime Projects*: "Guy H. Blanchett [sic] was well-respected for his expert ability in technical surveying, but he was a cold, aloof man who did not mix socially with any of us on his crew, White or Native. There was no racial discrimination but neither was there any human compassion. He was a hard man to work for and the living conditions only made the job worse."

Guy had been through such conditions many times before, and while he did not enjoy the heat and the bugs, he knew how to survive without complaint with a toughness that comes from experience. He was more than three times the age of the boys, and while his aloofness may have been a strategy to cope with the normal fatigue under the circumstances, he had always been a solitary, self-contained man, hard-working, but fair. However, while his strategy and provisioning had worked well for him up to 1920, he had not taken into account how much the world had changed in a quarter of a century.

On August 2 the boys quit. Guy was understandably upset, and threatened to withhold their pay, hoping it might change their minds, but when that didn't work he gave them their unemployment insurance books and enough food to get to the American base at Mills Lake. They soon found work on a riverboat going north to Norman Wells, and on their return south they passed close enough to the survey party, now across the Mackenzie River and west of Mills Lake, to wave to their former workmates and they saw that there had been no other defections.[2]

The survey party continued north as far as it could go in the season, but the whole experience had been disappointing for Guy, especially compared with his early years of surveying base lines. When he returned home at the end of the season, he informed the surveyor-general that he would not be continuing the survey down the Mackenzie River in the following year, but instead would write the British Columbia examinations to qualify him to work in his home province. On receiving Guy's decision, the surveyor-general wrote, "I think you are courageous to undertake to write exams [at this stage in your life]."[3]

Why would Guy, then over sixty, have such a strong desire to continue working?

Many people who had been affected by the Great Depression were forever marked by the need for security. In fact, Guy's attitude to work is neatly summed up in a letter to a former colleague in Ottawa in 1948, when, at age sixty-four, he commented that he could sense the presence of "retirement crouching behind the door."[4]

With the BC qualification, Guy was now able to add the letters BCLS to the DLS behind his name and, for the first time since the end of 1938, he was at home in Victoria for more than fleeting visits.[5] Over the next few years Guy had enough work to satisfy him, with surveying contracts on Vancouver Island and for mining companies in the interior of British Columbia and the Yukon.

With his many contacts, Guy was kept well informed of developments in the oil and mining industry throughout the west. The discovery of vast oil reserves in the Leduc field in Alberta in 1947, followed during the next two years by equally large discoveries in several areas south of Edmonton, created a stir in the oil pipeline industry. The Interprovincial Pipeline, built to take oil east to the refineries at Sarnia, Ontario, was completed in 1950, but

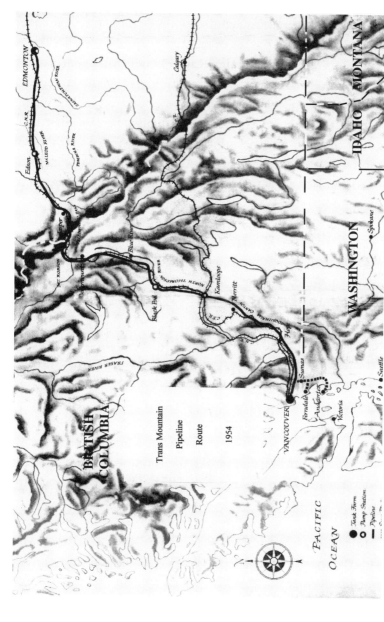

Map 11. The route of the Trans Mountain Pipeline, taken from the endpapers of The Building of Trans Mountain, published in 1954 by the Trans Mountain Oil Pipe Line Company, now part of Kinder Morgan Company Calgary, Alberta, and Houston, Texas.

British Columbia still faced the much higher cost of bringing its oil in by tanker from California. With North Korea's invasion of South Korea in June of 1950, once again the supply of oil to the west coast became more urgent as a matter of security.

A group of Canadian and American oil companies approached S.D. Bechtel, head of Bechtel Corporation, the giant American construction company, with a proposal to build a pipeline from Edmonton to the west coast. While this would be less than half the length of the Interprovincial Pipeline — 1800 miles — it would have to cross two formidable mountain barriers, the Canadian Rockies and the Coastal Range. Mr. S.D. Bechtel called a meeting of the interested oil producers in San Francisco in December 1950. Among them was H.H. Hall, from the Canol Project, who knew something of the terrain to be crossed. Hall had made a close inspection of the topographical maps, and had decided that there were only two possible routes: one, an all-Canadian route by way of the Yellowhead Pass to Vancouver; the other, crossing the Rockies through the Crow's Nest Pass, and dipping down into the United States to finish in Seattle. Hall and four other engineers travelled the two routes, parts of it by car and other parts by train, giving consideration to everything that would be required to build the pipeline, material, equipment, legal matters, financing, etc., and reported their findings to Bechtel early in January. Their choice — one hundred miles shorter and with lower mountain passes — was the all-Canadian route.[6] And, to make the route work, they needed an all-Canadian surveyor. In February, 1951, Hall wrote to his old (now 67) friend Blanchet:

> Dear Guy:
>
> It looks now as if I would have some pipeline reconnaissance to do in Western Canada in the near future, and I am wondering if you might be available to help me do it....The work so far authorized is strictly temporary but time, as usual, is very important, I would like to have a quick answer from you. Probably a telegram would be best...

In the last few minutes, I have just come from
Dick Finnie's office…he sent his best regards to you,
just as I do.

Harry Hall[7]

In his previous work of finding the route for the Canol pipeline,
Guy had built a solid reputation for making decisions and standing
behind them, and had worked closely with H.H. Hall to their
mutual respect. Hall having just finished work in Saudi Arabia on
the Trans-Arabian pipeline was intending to retire on a ranch he
was building near San Francisco, but like Guy Blanchet he was
restless. After a month of retirement he had opened a consulting
office in San Francisco where Bechtel had found him. Dick Finnie,
another old friend, was head of the public relations department of
the Bechtel Corporation.

Guy's assignment was to travel the entire 700 miles of the proposed
route and make a ground investigation at certain points where the
situation was obscure with regard to elevation or terrain, or where there
was a choice of locations. Blanchet left Vancouver at the beginning of
March and, although winter conditions somewhat restricted the work,
he had completed the first part of his reconnaissance by the end of
May. Most of the route was accessible by train or car, and he could
examine the most problematic areas on foot.

In reporting on the section from Hope to Kamloops, Guy's
laconic words, "This was examined from the railway speeder,"
conveys nothing of the experience or of the country through
which he had travelled.[8] In travelling through the Coquihalla
Canyon he was using the final and most difficult section of the
Kettle Valley Railway, opened in 1916. Within those thirty miles
was possibly the most expensive two miles of railway construction
ever undertaken, involving forty-three bridges, thirteen tunnels,
and sixteen snowsheds, to say nothing of the tons of earth and rock
to be moved, by the sweat and toil of immigrant workers, mainly
without benefit of machinery. Long stretches of the line were
located on perpendicular rock bluffs, three to five hundred feet
above the roaring Coquihalla River, and it was known worldwide as

Blanchet, Cliff Amarantes and Fred Ott, walking the rails during the exploration of the route for the Trans Mountain Pipeline, 1951.

a masterpiece of railroad engineering. Sadly, in 1959 — just eight years after Guy travelled it — the railway was permanently closed when heavy rains washed out the line in four places, and the cost of repair was prohibitive.[9]

Along that stretch of line, the railway stations — really just sidings — were all named for characters in Shakespeare's plays, an ironic touch of gentility for the railway traversing one of the most rugged regions on earth. At those sidings, Guy was able to get off the speeder, and examine the terrain on foot to see where the pipeline could be located. The speeder, used by railwaymen to inspect the track, was open to the elements, and may have been propelled by a small diesel or by a hand-pump — in either case, it was not a comfortable way to travel. After viewing the land, he recommended that the pipeline be buried at the bottom of the canyon between Portia and Romeo (station names now discontinued) to safeguard it from landslides. Looking for an alternative to this route, Guy studied the possibility of using Boston Bar Creek — now the route of the Coquihalla Highway — and he must have done this entirely on foot because there were no other means of doing it at the time. Although he does not mention it in his report, one can only presume that he was able to stay in the small huts used by railway section hands along the route.[10]

Between Hope and Coquihalla, in a distance of thirty miles there is a gain in elevation of 3,750 feet, followed by a sharp drop of 750 feet down to Brodie seven miles farther east. At Brodie, Guy was able to continue on a branch line up to Merritt, on the Coldwater River, finding few difficult sections. Northeast of Merritt lies the long, narrow Nicola Lake and Guy examined both sides to find the best way past, but it was only when he was able to study aerial photographs of the whole area that he could determine a direct route for the pipeline.

As he followed the Thompson River north from Kamloops by car, he had to consider which side of the river was more favourable. In places the valley is so narrow that there was room only for the highway, and he examined the ground carefully to find space for the pipeline. Further north, to Valemount he could only view the route from the train, and saw that the steep sides of the valley left little choice of location.

While the route would be through narrow mountain valleys across most of British Columbia, the section between Hope, on the Fraser River, up through the valleys of the Coquihalla and Coldwater rivers to Kamloops would be the most difficult part. By the middle of May, Guy reported that he had completed the basic reconnaissance as far as Kamloops and that he had made a preliminary investigation from Kamloops north to Valemount at the head of the Thompson River valley.

Knowing that from Valemount to Jasper there was a passable road, and beyond Jasper to Edmonton, a good highway, leaving only the problems of river crossings and stretches of muskeg to be considered, Guy had completed his preliminary job and was in Kamloops by the middle of May, waiting to hear whether the consortium had made the decision whether or not to build the pipeline.

The consortium of companies, meanwhile, had applied to the Canadian Government for a charter to create a company to build a pipeline over the proposed route. This was granted on March 31, 1951, and the Trans Mountain Oil Pipe Line Company was founded. It was a public company, with Canadian Bechtel and Imperial Oil subscribing for half the shares, and inviting five major oil companies to subscribe for the other half. When a more detailed study of the route was completed, and safe locations on stable ground were established, a vote would be taken by shareholders on the decision to proceed.[11]

The building of the Trans Mountain Pipeline was a very different proposition to the building of the Canol pipeline. It was an entirely private venture, and the principals financing and constructing it had to be satisfied that it was feasible and economically sound. This was in complete contrast to Canol, which had been initiated as a wartime emergency measure with financing from the deep pockets of the American Government. There was another important difference. Canol was built across unsurveyed Crown land, and geography was the only restriction on the location. Because Trans Mountain would be crossing cities and villages, farms and parks, following railways and highways, always on land that had been previously surveyed, the pipeline survey had to be tied in to the existing surveys and, where necessary, the legal rights-of-way had to be negotiated with private landowners.

By the middle of July 1951, Guy received a further letter from his friend, Harry Hall:

> Your comments on the reconnaissance location were very interesting to me. I feel that your work in exploring these cut-offs has been a very material contribution to the location of this pipe line. You can without doubt be of further aid to the project as an employee of the Canadian branch of the Bartlett Company [contracted to survey and map the line]... It is my own idea that your field of usefulness might be somewhat wider than the direct survey of the line. I have in mind map and ownership procurement and contact with engineering officials of the various

provinces…if the Bartlett Company is going to handle right-of-way procurement as well as survey.

In closing, I want to express my sincere appreciation for the excellent work which you have done in reconnoitring this pipe line.[12]

The next order of business was to have Guy's proposed route studied by groups consisting of engineers and surveyors, using both maps and aerial photographs. Each group was headed by a pipeline specialist — or "pipeliner" — emphasizing the difference in technique between the construction of pipelines and other projects such as railways or highways. Because pumping stations are an integral part of the whole structure for moving liquids over long distances, pipelines are able to go up much steeper gradients than roadbeds and can descend straight down canyon walls. They can also bend around much sharper corners.

While the six groups each covered sections of the entire route on foot, flagging the most feasible line, Guy examined two problem areas in the Thompson River valley. When accommodation was unavailable, Blanchet and the other surveyors were provided with a "boarding" train. The early onset of winter in 1951 added to their problems.

From the Thompson River, Guy then moved on to another difficult stretch going east from the Yellowhead Pass in Alberta through Jasper National Park in Alberta where the Miette valley is either wide and swampy or narrow and fully occupied by the river.[13] The Canadian National Railway track was on one side of the valley and the highway had been built on the ground of the abandoned Canadian Northern on the other side. After working carefully through this thirty-mile area, Guy finally settled on a location for the pipeline.

In the middle of November, work moved into high gear with the firm objective: to build "The Big Inch" — a 24-inch pipeline — and there was a time limit to complete the work. In addition to teams of surveyors, now working on the actual line, there were hundreds of men operating bulldozers, tractors, cranes and numerous other machines needed in such specialized and dangerous work. At one place one of the four tractors, linked together to haul a heavy crane up a steep hill, broke loose and slid back down the hill for 500 feet, gathering speed as it went. The operator jumped to safety, but his tractor hit a second tractor on the way down, jettisoning its operator into the air. The operator survived uninjured, but the runaway tractor was completely demolished.[14]

Working ahead of the actual construction, as always, Guy was far removed from the hurly-burly of heavy machinery. His work with the survey company was as chief of the legal survey work in British Columbia, securing rights-of-way for the pipeline to pass through privately owned land. Other surveyors also working ahead of the construction mapped the exact route as Blanchet had located it. In his final work for Trans Mountain, Guy was commissioned by the surveyor-general of Canada to be in charge of making sure that the whole pipeline was marked with permanent survey monuments every six miles and tied in to the established national survey grid. On the Alberta section — where Guy had done much of his work in the early years of his career — this was not difficult to do, but in British Columbia many of the original corner posts were of wood and had either rotted away or broken off. The work of searching, resurveying and marking more than 200 miles of the pipeline was not completed until late in November of 1953.[15]

While the work on the Canol pipeline had been more difficult and demanding, the Trans Mountain pipeline was the pinnacle of Blanchet's career. Canol, the first pipeline built across a mountain range, was the prototype, showing what was possible. Canol delivered oil for less than a year before it was abandoned. The Trans Mountain continues right up to the present day to provide all the petroleum used on the west coast of British Columbia.

With the completion of the Trans Mountain pipeline, Guy celebrated his seventieth birthday and retired. The Trans Mountain pipeline was a fitting conclusion to fifty years of work undertaken mostly in the North and the West, all of it interesting and challenging.

THIRTEEN — WRITING, FRIENDSHIP, TRAVEL: 1954–1966

For years Guy had actively resisted retirement, but the successful completion of the Trans Mountain pipeline found him ready to settle down and enjoy the home he shared with his wife and his sister in Victoria. Guy would have a chance to sail his sloop, *Ptarmigan*, which was moored at a marina near Capi's woodland cottage, and would have the pleasure of seeing something of her family, now grown up, along with nieces and nephews from other parts of the country when they came to the west coast.

Capi's cottage was situated on the most easterly point of a peninsula, roughly one mile square, not far from Swartz Bay, the current terminal for the BC ferry service to Vancouver. Her youngest son, David, after completing his first year at the University of British Columbia, had joined the army at the beginning of the Second World War. At the end of the war, David returned to university for a year, but dropped out when he became involved in building a house for a friend. Realizing his own home had become dilapidated, he and his mother worked together to tear it down and build an attractive bungalow overlooking the sea. Fiercely independent and stubborn, Capi had always refused to have a telephone and, when David needed to phone anyone, he went to their nearest neighbour, a mile away on the southern point of the peninsula. These neighbours, Raymond and Marigold Patterson, had arrived from Alberta just after the end of the war, and were an adventurous pair who had crossed the mountains on horseback in early winter on the way to British Columbia. Their daughter, Janet, equally adventurous, had recently returned from taking part in a trail drive delivering sixty-two horses north to Telegraph Creek on the Stikine River, involving a difficult ride through the interior of British Columbia. It wasn't long before David Blanchet fell in love with Janet Patterson and they were married in 1948. This became the source of a new and rewarding friendship for Guy.[1]

In 1954, the year that Guy retired, R.M. Patterson published his first book, *Dangerous River*, the story of his exploration of the South Nahanni River in 1927, and wintering there with a partner, Gordon Matthews, in 1928-29. This was a tale of high adventure, introducing the glories of the Nahanni to the Canadian public. It has never gone out of print. As the friendship between Blanchet and Patterson developed, the two men would settle of an evening into comfortable easy chairs in Guy's book-lined den, a glass of whisky in hand, and the stories would flow. Both men had lived adventurous lives, Blanchet ranging over the northern prairies and the Northwest Territories, while Patterson laid claim to the southern Yukon, northern British Columbia and the Rockies. Over the next dozen years, Patterson would write four more books about his years of ranching in the Alberta foothills and about some of his later canoeing explorations of northern British Columbia, weaving into them the travels of early fur traders, prospectors and surveyors.

Their shared interests embraced the tales of earlier travellers in the North, and while Patterson did the detailed research of the historic fur-trader, Samuel Black, Blanchet contributed information gathered on the ground where Black had traded.[2] In 1955, a new volume in the Hudson's Bay Record Society series, *Samuel Black's Journal of his Rocky Mountain Expedition of 1824,* dealt with the journey made by an early Hudson's Bay trader to assess the fur resources of the wild country of the Finlay and Parsnip rivers in northern British Columbia. Using knowledge of the area gained from his own canoe exploration, Raymond Patterson wrote the long and scholarly introduction to the book. Guy reviewed the book in *The Beaver* the following year, praising Patterson's introduction and his illumination of obscure passages of the journal in the footnotes. In two sentences of the review Guy could have been writing of his own experiences and journals: "It may have been lack of companionship that led Black to resort to his journal which must

Courtesy of Richard Blanchet

Retirement at last. Blanchet in his own sailboat, Ptarmigan, *off Sidney, British Columbia, with an unidentified friend, 1960.*

have occupied many long hours"; and "A journal of an explorer often reveals the man as much as his travels."[3]

In the same issue of *The Beaver* in which the review appeared, Patterson contributed an article on the character of Samuel Black, and Guy's colleague, the surveyor F.C. Swannell, wrote an article based on his survey of the same area, made ninety years after Black's original trip. It was a banner issue of the magazine, bringing together three intrepid modern explorers from the Victoria area.

In retirement, writing became central to Guy's life. With his new leisure, in 1954 he gave his imagination full rein and wrote the story about John Hornby and Critchell-Bullock, entitled "The Letter," quoted in an earlier chapter. Guy sent the manuscript to George Douglas who commented on it with pleasure in a letter of March 31, 1954.[4] Hornby would have been very much on the minds of both men at the time. George Whalley, a professor from Queen's University in Kingston, Ontario, was in the midst of writing a book about Hornby. His research involved correspondence with Guy, as well as lengthy interviews with George Douglas in Lakefield. Douglas, having had old memories stirred, wrote long letters to Guy talking over his feelings about Hornby and about the forthcoming book. When "The Letter" was submitted to *The Beaver*, it was rejected, but after Whalley's book, *The Legend of John Hornby*, was published in 1962, they published Guy's article in 1963 and also his review of the book.[5]

Several other articles for *The Beaver* flowed from Guy's pen based on his early survey experiences, and he was also frequently contributing a column of reminiscences to the Sunday edition of the Victoria newspaper, *The Daily Colonist*. In 1960, the Macmillan Company of Toronto published his only book, *Search in the North*. No correspondence exists to indicate whether he had initiated this project or whether the publisher had sought him out. While we do not know how much time was involved in writing the book, in a letter dated August 4, 1958, George Douglas mentioned that John Gray, the editor from Macmillan had been visiting him in Lakefield and discussing Guy's manuscript.[6] The editorial revisions of the manuscript required Guy to drop the impersonal style he had to use when writing government reports and put himself clearly in the action.

In just under 200 pages, Guy told the story of his year spent on the coast of Hudson Bay in charge of the aerial prospecting base for Colonel C.D.H. MacAlpine, and the details of the misadventures in the aerial search for MacAlpine's two missing planes. It is written without hyperbole, requiring readers to use their imaginations to appreciate the hazards involved in the eighteen-month-long saga. A review in *Canadian Literature* praises the writer for his controlled sense of drama, and for the modesty and authenticity of the writing. "Modesty" is also the word used by the reviewer in *The Beaver,* who notes the casualness with which Guy wrote of the eleven days spent in the depths of winter on Aylmer Lake, with the pilot and mechanic of their wrecked plane, at the end of the search for the missing planes. Blanchet's impression of the awesome beauty of the northern landscape and his deep admiration for the local group of Inuit are strong features of the book, achieved with sincerity and without resorting to "colourful" writing.[7]

Possibly in celebration of completing the work on his book, Guy bought a ticket on the Japanese ship, *Hikawa Maru*, and sailed alone from Seattle to Yokohama, Japan, in March of 1959.[8] It had been twenty years since he made the trip across the Pacific to Fiji and New Zealand and he was excited at the prospect of a new adventure. While Eileen had sometimes gone abroad when Guy was in the North, she was no longer interested in travel. Her eyesight was beginning to fail and she loved their comfortable home. Guy was gone for nearly three months, most of his time in Japan spent in the mountains in central Japan, staying in a *ryokan,* or traditional Japanese guest house, away from modernization and other tourists. In a letter to Dick Finnie, he mentioned that his "special little maid, Keiko san, was charming and cared for me like a 'mother.' " He quickly adapted to Japanese food and chopsticks, and agreed with the Japanese view that "Westerners are Barbarians." While he was there, the volcano Asama erupted and several minor earthquakes occurred, adding to the interest.[9]

As he wrote to Dick Finnie, "Writing interests me regardless of the results." After the success of his book, his publisher suggested another book based on Guy's experiences as a surveyor, and Guy began work on a manuscript.[10] He had two possible titles, "These Fifty Years," and the more romantic sounding, "Beyond the Ranges." While Guy had always done his own typing, in 1966 he hired two young women to help him with this new manuscript. His eyes had developed cataracts, and he underwent an operation to have them removed in 1966 — a more critical operation in those days than it is now. Again writing to Dick Finnie, "The cataract operation was a partial success, pretty good at my age [82] and my philosophy is 'with acceptance comes peace'. He could still use the typewriter but he had to give up driving his car.[11]

Work on his memoirs progressed slowly, but in June, Guy suffered a serious heart attack and was in hospital for several weeks. When he was allowed to go home, he enjoyed walking about his own house, sitting outside in the sun and doing some work on his book. But in August he had another attack, which was fatal.[12]

Guy and Eileen's home had always been a welcoming place for their many nephews and nieces. Eileen was the glue that held their home together while Guy was away on his long working trips. Their home had been the setting for the wedding of his nephew Eric, whose wife remembered Eileen as "A dear," and Guy, with "a smile like the sun coming out" that could light up any room he entered.[13] At the time of Guy's death, Eric helped Eileen to collect and sort all of Guy's papers and photographs and deposit them in the provincial archives in Victoria.

Through his published writing, and particularly through his personal diaries, a portrait of the man begins to emerge. Those who worked with him knew him as a brilliant organizer, careful, competent and decisive. He had the mental stamina to match his physical strength and he would let no obstacle stand in the way of finishing the work he set out to do. In a tight spot, he was unflappable and exactly the right companion for the occasion. Guy Blanchet was also a man of contrasts. He had a complex personality, his cool, aloof exterior, covered strong emotions, and his private inner life was sometimes a turmoil of doubt and self-recrimination. Calm as he appeared on the surface, he had a restless spirit, always looking for new challenges, new scenes. Even on an arduous survey, a designated rest day in camp would find him eager for the next morning's move. The books he carried on his survey trips, often literary classics, contrasted surprisingly with the primitive life he enjoyed when the opportunity arose. The totally masculine milieu of his working life gave him an enhanced appreciation of women as a civilizing influence, and he always enjoyed being in their company.

Guy Blanchet's working life mirrored the developments taking place in the Canadian North in the first half of the twentieth century. He had a reputation as a first-rate surveyor and a superb map-maker who kept pace with the technological advances of the day. In his early survey work, using transit and chain, he marked out meridians and base lines throughout the northern boreal forests of Alberta and Saskatchewan, as part of the topographical grid. When he moved on to mapping parts of the Mackenzie and Liard rivers, the perimeter and islands of Great Slave Lake, and large areas of the Barrens in his search for the headwaters of the Coppermine and Thelon rivers, wireless signals had become the means of checking locations. It was always thrilling for him to set off into an area of the North where no map existed, following river courses and using his observations of the land forms to find his way, accompanied by a Native guide whenever possible. Early in his career he learned Cree so he could hear the stories connected to the land, and when he spent the year on the coast of Hudson Bay he learned some Inuktitut. In the last part of his career, finding and surveying routes for oil pipelines, he was doing work which could not have been imagined when his career began.

His work involved constant travel, and Blanchet used every form of transport: in the early years, dog team, pack horse, canoe and the Athabasca Brigade; later, train, automobile, Hudson's Bay steamer and airplane; and always, miles and miles of walking. His knowledge of the written accounts of earlier travellers in the North enhanced his own work, and he was sometimes able to clarify obscure points, such as deciphering place names in the journey by Samuel Hearne. His friendships, including John Hornby, George Douglas, Richard Finnie, J.C. Critchell-Bullock, Raymond Patterson, and pioneer pilots, Punch Dickins and Matt Berry, constituted an elite group whose northern travels are a pivotal part of the story of the Canadian North in the first half of the twentieth century.

Notes

Introduction

1.　Thomson, Don W., *Men and Meridians: The History of Surveying and Mapping in Canada* Vol.1 (Ottawa: Queen's Printer, 1969) 1–3.
2.　From the Web site of the British Columbia Land Surveyors Association: http://www.bc.landsurveyors.bc.ca, accessed on April 24, 2007.

Prologue

1.　British Columbia Archives (BCA), MS-0498, box 9, 10, Drafts of "Beyond the Ranges" and "These Fifty Years," unpublished memoirs.

Chapter 1: Early Life: 1884–1906

1.　Eggleston, Wilfrid, *The Queen's Choice: A Story of Canada's Capital* (Ottawa: Queen's Printer, 1961), 153
2.　Information from Janet Blanchet.
3.　*Dictionnaire généalogique des familles du Québec* (Montréal: Les Presses de l'université de Montréal,1983) 113–14; Répetoire des actes de baptême, mariage, sépulture et desrecensements du Québec ancien (Montréal, PUM, 1980) 7 volumes.
4.　Jean de Biencourt de Poutrincourt was the founder of the first colony at Port-Royal (now Annapolis Royal) in Nova Scotia. In 1606, he became the lieutenant-governor of Acadia, establishing good relations with the Native Peoples through his fair and just treatment of them.
5.　*Dictionary of Canadian Biography*, Vol. 1, 367–68.
6.　BCA, MS-0498, box 9, 10 and 12; Civil Service Lists of Canada, 1885, 1886, and up to 1914.
7.　*Ottawa City Directory*, (Ottawa, Might's Directory Co.) 1867.
8.　Letter from Frances Blanchet to David Blanchet, June 8, 1976, courtesy of Cathy Converse.
9.　Eggleston, 153
10.　Munsey's Bridge may have been named for James Munce, one of the early settlers who arrived in the area at the beginning of the nineteenth century.

11. Eggleston, *The Queen's Choice*; Woods, *Ottawa: The Capital of Canada*; and Bond, *The City on the Ottawa*.

12. The Dominion Experimental Farm, founded in 1886, consisted of 446 acres of agricultural land on the western edge of the city. The farm was intended to be an agricultural laboratory. It has grown to 1200 acres and is the largest farm in the world entirely surrounded by city.

13. Bond, *City on the Ottawa*, 13–14. The poem, found in Bond's book, is from Arthur Bourinot's book, *To and Fro on the Earth*, self-published in 1963. The poem was quoted in full by Bond with the kind permission of the author. Bourinot died in 1969.

14. Porter, Prof J.B. (Prof. of Mining Engineering at McGill) "The education of mining engineers" in *Journal of the Canadian Mining Institute*, Vol. IX, 1906, 5–10.

15. BCA, MS-0498, box 1, file #1. The title of the paper was "Trans-Continental Transportation."

16. BCA, MS-0498, box 9, 10; Web site, http://www.ghosttownpix.com/alberta/Graphics/LilleTownMap.jpg, accessed on March 23, 2004.

17. BCA, MS-0498, box 9, 10; Web site for the Frank Slide Interpretive Centre: http://www.frankslide.com/info.html, accessed on March 23, 2004.

18. BCA MS-0498, box 9,10.

Chapter 2: The Surveyor: 1906–1919

1. Brown, Robert Craig and Ramsay Cook, *Canada 1869–1921: A Nation Transformed* (Toronto: McClelland & Stewart, 1974), 56.

2. Gunter's chain, named for Edmund Gunter, is a measuring device, consisting of 100 heavy gauge wire links, with a loop at each end. The chain can be folded up, link by link, into a bundle that can be held in the hand. The chain is sixty-six feet long, and that distance is termed a chain.

3. Unless otherwise noted, much of the material in this chapter is based on Blanchet's unpublished memoirs in BCA MS-0498, box 9, 10.

4. In 1905, the North West Mounted Police became the Royal North West Mounted police in recognition of their service in the Boer War. In 1920, the name was changed again, this time to the Royal Canadian Mounted Police (RCMP).

5. Caption in Blanchet photograph album, courtesy of Richard Blanchet, a great-nephew.

6. The Geological Survey of Canada (GSC), one of the oldest government organizations and the first scientific establishment in Canada, was founded by the Province of Canada to investigate the rich natural resources of the country, with a view to a future mining industry. Following Confederation in 1867, and especially after 1870 when the Hudson's Bay Company ceded the huge land mass

of Rupert's Land to the Canadian government, the activity of the GSC increased dramatically as teams of scientists undertook long, arduous and adventurous journeys by canoe into the northwest using the rivers as their highways.

7. MacGregor, J.G., *Vision of an Ordered Land: The Story of the Dominion Land Survey* (Saskatoon: Western Prairie Producer books, 1967) ix.

8. In 1793, Alexander Mackenzie undertook his epic journey to the Pacific Ocean, searching for a useful overland route to the sea, after the frustration of his first attempt in 1789 when he reached the Arctic Ocean. After a journey, made difficult and dangerous by powerful rivers and some hostile Native Peoples, he reached an island off the coast and painted the following inscription on a large rock: "Alexander Mackenzie, 1793, from Canada by land."

9. MacGregor, 39, 82.

10. As a result of Britain having dominant control of the Suez Canal, Egypt had become practically a protectorate of the British Government. In 1883, in the Egyptian Sudan, a leader calling himself the Mahdi, had gathered together the tribes of the interior and was attempting to take control of the area. The British, under General Charles George Gordon (1833–83), wished to withdraw their garrison from the Sudan but were surrounded by hostile forces at Khartoum. The only possible way to send reinforcements to assist General Gordon was up the Nile River. In 1884, a force of 377 volunteer Canadian boatmen was recruited to man a fleet of whale boats to convey the troops up the river from Cairo to Khartoum, past six sets of rapids. For their services, the Canadian boatmen were awarded the British War Medal as well as an Egyptian award known as the Khedive's Star. The Canadian initiative was successful, but General Gordon did not survive the siege of Khartoum.

11. Mallory, Enid, *Coppermine: The Far North of George M. Douglas* (Peterborough: Broadview Press, 1989) Chapter 2.

12. The permissible deviation was one foot per mile. Interview with Bob Parr, surveyor of Elliott and Parr, on April 13, 2007.

13. Logan, Robert, "The 19th Base-line West of the 4th Meridian," in *Alberta Historical Review*, Autumn, 1960, 1–7.

14. Public Records Office: Ontario Marriage Certificate; Ottawa Street Directories, 1891-99; Ontario Cemetery Finding Aid; Canadian Imperial Bank of Commerce Archives; Saint John Daily Telegraph, April 10, 1902.

15. Taken frrom Blanchet's photo album, courtesy of Richard Blanchet.

16. The Churchill Brigade was the Hudson's Bay Company's answer to the North West Company's northern supply route. For years the North West Company (NWC) sent its flotillas of *canot de maître* west through lakes Huron and Superior to Fort William, where

goods were transferred to the smaller north canoes, to continue on routes that eventually reached the northern posts. The Hudson's Bay Company, based at York Factory on Hudson Bay, had preferred to let the Native people do the travelling. But with fierce competition from the NWC, they had to develop a better method. Consequently, they sent their men up the swift-flowing Nelson River in York boats to Norway House at the top of Lake Winnipeg, and westward from there on the Churchill River.

17.   Samuel Black, one of the most powerful fur traders of the North West Company, was reluctantly hired by George Simpson to work for the Hudson's Bay Company after the amalgamation of the two companies in 1821. He made a difficult exploration of the little-known mountainous area northwest of the Peace River in British Columbia, searching for new areas for the fur trade. That area was not considered fruitful and he was assigned to a dangerous post among the Nez Percés, where he was shot dead. His comprehensive diary was published many years later by the Hudson's Bay Record Society.

Chapter 3: North of Sixty: 1920–1923

1.   BCA, MS-0498, box 9, 10.

2.   Molson, K.M., *Pioneering in Canadian Air Transport* (Winnipeg: James Richardson & Sons Ltd., 1974) 2.

3   John Franklin led two Arctic land trips on which they wintered over. On the first trip in 1820, they travelled north to the ocean to map the Arctic coast. However, they explored too late in the season and on their return up the Coppermine River, nine of the expedition died of starvation and other causes. Franklin returned in 1825, wintered at a fort they constructed on Great Bear Lake, and again explored and mapped the Arctic coast, this time with no loss of life.

4.   Lieutenant George Back took part in both of Franklin's two land journeys, and on the first expedition he made an heroic 1,000 mile winter trek out to the nearest Hudson's Bay post for supplies to save the total group from starvation. In 1833, Commander George Back returned to the Arctic to lead an expedition to search for Sir John Ross, whose ship had been missing in the Arctic waters for four years. He built Fort Reliance at the east end of Great Slave Lake as his wintering quarters, and as he was about to set out on his rescue mission in the spring, he received word that Ross had successfully returned to England. Back then mounted an expedition to explore the northeastern Arctic, making the first descent of the Great Fish River (later named the Back River in his honour) and returned up river safely in the same season, with his crew intact. He returned to England the following year to great acclaim.

5   Father Emil Fortune Stanilas Joseph Petitot was an Oblate missionary who arrived in the North at Great Slave Lake in 1862. He was much

interested in the geography of the country, and during his missionary journeys he explored, mapped and wrote about the area between the Mackenzie and Liard rivers. In 1878, he discovered a tributary of the Liard River, which was named the Petitot in his honour.

6. BCA, MS-0498, box 12, file 27; Hoyle, "The Canoeist's Unique Northern legacy, in *Canada's River Heritage,* (John Marsh, Bruce Hodgins, Erik Hanson eds.) (Peterborough: Trent University, 1966) 64–67.

7. In 1914, at the urging of Vilhjalmur Stefansson, the Canadian government mounted a large scientific expedition to explore many aspects of the Arctic. Scientists from a variety of disciplines, including biology, anthropology, physics and geography were hired, along with surveyors. While originally Stefansson was to have been in charge, a co-leader was added in the person of Dr. R.M. Anderson, whose speciality was biology. The beginning of the expedition coincided with the outbreak of the First World War, and it finished just before the war's end in the summer of 1918. While much good work was done, there was also disaster and tragedy. The scientists sailed north from Victoria on an Arctic whaler, the *Karluk,* which became frozen into the ice north of Alaska. Stefansson and a handful of scientists were on shore when it happened. Anderson and a few others were sailing on a smaller ship that got through, but the *Karluk,* stuck on an ice floe, was carried westward. Before the ship was destroyed by the ice, Captain Bob Bartlett of Newfoundland, got those remaining off the ship and led them across the ice to Wrangel Island. With the support of one Inuit, Bartlett made an incredible trek to Siberia, where he found a boat to take them to Alaska to organize a rescue party for the survivors. While many did survive the long ordeal, unfortunately a number of the scientists and crew were lost. One interesting outcome of the expedition was that Stefansson discovered several previously unknown islands.

8. Whalley, George, *The Legend of John Hornby* (Toronto: Macmillan, 1962, Laurentian Library, 1977) 25–26.

9. George Blondin's book, *Yamoria, the Lawmaker: Stories of the Dene,* contains many stories relating to the animals and the Dene people.

10. Ernest Thompson Seton describes his 1907 journey with E.A. Preble and provides many references to Souci Beaulieu and his relatives in his book, *The Arctic Prairies.*

Chapter 4: Exploration: 1924–1925

1. Discarded correspondence files, Dept. of Energy Mines and Resources, courtesy of R.H. Cockburn.

2. BCA, MS-0498, box 5.

3. BCA, MS-0498, box 1, Correspondence; Whalley, 179.

4. BCA, MS-0498, box 5.

5. BCA, MS-0498, box 9,10; and box 12, #15, "Man Overboard."
6. BCA, MS-0498, box 5; Blanchet, "Narrative of a Journey to the Source of the Coppermine River" in *Bulletin of the Geographical Society of Philadelphia*, Vol. XXIV, Jan.–Oct. 1926, 163–77; Blanchet, "An Exploration into the Northern Plains North and East of Great Slave Lake, Including the Source of the Coppermine River," in *The Canadian Field-Naturalist*, Vols. XXXVIII, XXXIX, Dec. 1924, Jan., Feb., 1925.
7. On October 18, 1932, Ernest Thompson Seton began a correspondence with the Department of the Interior and the surveyor general, protesting that his mapping and naming of locations in the Lockhart River basin, which he had registered with the Royal Geographical Society, London, had been ignored. The source is discarded correspondence files, Dept. of Energy, Mines and Resources, courtesy of Prof. R.H. Cockburn.
8. In 1855, James Anderson, a chief factor of the Hudson's Bay Company at Fort Resolution on Great Slave Lake, along with James Stewart and eight others, made a trip down the Great Fish (or Back) River to search for members of the Franklin expedition that had been missing since 1847. They reached Chantrey Inlet but found no evidence of survivors and returned up the river.
9. BCA, MS-0498, box 1, Correspondence, Letter Malvina Bolus, editor, *The Beaver*, in 1953; Whalley, 194–95.
10. E-mail from the Royal Geographical Society, London, Sept. 12, 2005.
11. BCA, MS-0498, box 3, Taltson Journals, 1–3; Blanchet, "New Light on Forgotten Trails in the Far Northwest," in *The Canadian Field-Naturalist*, Vol. XL, #4,5, April, May, 1926, 69–75; 96–99; Blanchet, "Into Unknown Country," in *The Beaver*, June 1950, 34–37.
12. Morse, Eric W., *Freshwater Saga: Memoirs of a Lifetime of Wilderness Canoeing in Canada* (Toronto: University of Toronto Press, 1987) 154. In 1972, Eric and Pamela Morse made a trip down the Taltson River, and on Nonacho Lake: "we spotted some faint writing made long ago by scraping off the black lichen which covered the slab. We could just make out 'G.B. 1924', Guy Blanchet, perhaps?" The date was actually 1925, but the writing was unclear.

Chapter 5: The Last Exploration on the Barrens: 1926

1. Whalley, 179.
2. BCA, MS-0498, box 1, Letter to Malvina Bolus, editor of *The Beaver*, 1953.
3. Whalley, 245–46.
4. BCA, MS-0498, box 12, #3.
5. Whalley, 257; National Archives Canada (NAC), MG-30, B95, Vol. 2., file #1, contains a voluminous correspondence between George Douglas and Guy Blanchet, especially active on the subject of John

Hornby during the time that George Whalley was interviewing Douglas and corresponding with Blanchet.

6. Whalley, 269–71.
7. BCA, MS-0498, box 12, file #3.
8. BCA, MS-0498, box 3, files #4–6, Dubawnt journals; Blanchet, "Crossing the Great Divide," in *The Bulletin of the Geographical Society of Philadelphia*, vol. XXV, Jan.-Oct. 1927, 141–53; Blanchet, "Thelewey-aza-yeth," in *The Beaver*, Sept. 1949, 8–11.
9. In 1893, Joseph Burr Tyrrell, with his brother James, made a long, exploratory canoe trip for the Geological Survey, beginning at Lake Athabasca and finishing on the Hudson Bay coast after the onset of winter. This was a region that had never been surveyed and their informative and accurate maps contained a wealth of new information on a previously unknown part of the country. James Tyrrell's book about the expedition, *Across the Sub-Arctic of Canada*, is a northern classic. J.B. Tyrrell lived a long and productive life and was inducted into the Mining Hall of Fame for his work as an explorer, cartographer, geologist and mining consultant.
10. Ontario Public Records Office.
11. Letter from Frances Blanchet to David Blanchet, June 8, 1976, courtesy of Cathy Converse.
12. Andrew, Ruby, "Sailing the Curve of Time," in *Beautiful British Columbia Magazine*, Winter, 1999, 30–35; Iglauer, Edith, "'Capi' Blanchet," in *The Strangers Next Door* (Madeira Park, B.C.: Harbour Publishing, 1991) 221–30.
13. E-mail letter from Judy Reid, granddaughter of Capi Blanchet, Nov. 19, 2005.
14. Stefansson Manuscripts, Rauner Special Collections Library, Dartmouth College, Hanover, New Hampshire, Correspondence between Stefansson and Blanchet, 1927.
15. BCA, MS-0498, box 1, file #1.
16. NAC, MG-30, B95, vol.2, file #1, Letter to Blanchet from George Douglas, October 11, 1945.

Chapter 6: Winter in the Arctic: 1928–1929

1. Unless otherwise noted this chapter is based on Blanchet's book, *Search in the North*.
2. BCA, MS-0498, box 1, letter from F.H. Peters, Surveyor-General.
3. Trent University Archives, unpublished memoir by Wallace MacAlpine; *The Canadian Who's Who*, 1936–37, 655.
4. Berton, Pierre, *Vimy* (Toronto: McClelland & Stewart, 1986) 51–66.
5. BCA, MS-0498, box 1, letter to Blanchet from Col. C.D.H. MacAlpine.
6. Thayer Lindsley had an uncanny perception of geology. He was able

to look at a geological map in three dimensions and quickly circle the location that had the greatest likelihood of producing valuable ore. In his own words, "To be a successful mine finder one must have determination, knowledge, tenacity [and] a rugged constitution to withstand the rigours of outdoor life, and enjoy overcoming obstacles of every description. Also, a little dash of imagination and enthusiasm is helpful." Lindsley either found or was involved in the development of Falconbridge Ltd., Sherritt Gordon, Giant Yellowknife, Canadian Malartic and United Keno Hill in Canada, as well as mines in Africa and Australia.

7. Smith, Philip, *Harvest from the Rock: A History of Mining in Ontario* (Toronto: Macmillan of Canada, 1986) 217–21.
8. Ibid, 233.
9. Molson, 41; Shaw, Margaret Mason, *Bush Pilots* (Toronto: Clarke, Irwin & Co., 1962) 59–63
10. Whalley, 317–18.
11. *Handbook of North American Indians* (Washington, D.C.: Smithsonian Institute, 1984) vol. 5, *The Arctic*, 448.
12. BCA, MS-0498, box 3, files, 7, 8, letters to Eileen Blanchet in the form of a diary.
13. Ibid.
14. Ibid.
15. Selected business pages of the *Globe and Mail* throughout the 1930s.

Chapter 7: Search and Rescue: 1929

1. This chapter is based on Blanchet's book, *Search in the North; Marooned in the Arctic: Diary of the Dominion Explorers' Expedition to the Arctic*, written and complied by Richard Pearce, editor of *The Northern Miner* (Toronto: s.n., 1931).
2. Molson, 78.
3. Ibid, 79.
4. Ibid, 80.
5. Pearce, Richard, *Marooned in the Arctic: Diary of the Dominion Explorers' Expedition to the Arctic* (Toronto: s. n., 1931) 59.
6. *Globe and Mail*, Dec. 1–7, 1929.

Chapter 8: The Thirties: 1930–1939

1. Website, Erasmus University, Rotterdam — School of Economics, http://people.few.eur.nl/smant/m-economics/crash1929.htm, Feb. 9, 2007.
2. Blanchet, "Conquering the Northern Air," in *The Beaver*, March 1939, 11–14.
3. Smith, 285.
4. BCA, box 11, #6, "The Coppermine Reaches the Ice Sea."
5. Although no one could have predicted it, this would be the last

complete Arctic trip made by *Baychimo*. The following year, she ventured too far east in the short season of open water and, late leaving the Arctic, was frozen in solidly on the Alaskan coast. Most of the passengers and crew were evacuated, while a skeleton crew, including the captain, built a shelter on shore to winter over and be ready to take control when break-up came the following summer. A fierce early winter blizzard swept the ship out to sea, still riding on the ice-pan to which it was attached, and for years after it could be seen, a ghost ship, patrolling the Arctic Ocean. By the time Blanchet wrote about seeing the *Baychimo*, he would have known of her fate. See Hoyle, Gwyneth, *Flowers in the Snow*, (Lincoln: University of Nebraska Press, 2001) 113–18.

6.   Shackleton, Kathleen, *Arctic Pilot: Life and Work on North Canadian Air Routes, the Experiences of Walter E. Gilbert, as told to Kathleen Shackleton* (Toronto: Thomas Nelson and Sons, 1940) 97–126.

7.   Personal information from Kay Hooke, niece of George Douglas.

8.   BCA, MS-0498, box 10, 130.

9.   BCA, MS-0498, box 1, letters from the Dept. of the Interior, and from Deputy Minister H.H. Rowatt, May 1, 1931.

10. Government of Canada, Sessional papers, #10, 1931.

11. BCA, MS-0498, box 1, May 1931.

12. BCA, MS-0498, box 5, notebooks and diaries of the years 1919-1952.

13. Ibid; Mallory, 198–217.

14. NAC, MG-30-B95, George Douglas, "Report on Explorations, Athabasca Lake and Great Slave Lake, Summer of 1935."

15. BCA, MS-0498, box 10 and box 1, 1936 letter regarding interview for the position at the Astronomical Observatory in Victoria at a salary of $1,440 per annum.

16. Denison, F.N., "Victoria, 'The City of Sunshine,' Capital of British Columbia and its Two Observatories," Victoria and Island Development Assoc., 1918.

17. Thomson, Vol. 3, 221. The article was in the *Journal of the Royal Astronomical Society of Canada*, Vol.23, 1929, 291.

18. Harper, W.E. and Blanchet, G.H. "The Spectroscopic Orbits of H.R. 5472," in *Publications of the Dominion Astrophysical Observatory*, Vol. 7, no.2, 99–104, 1938.

19. Beals, C.S. and Blanchet, G.H. "A Broad Absorption Line at λ 4430.5 of Possibly Interstellar Origin," in *Publication of the Astronomic Society of the Pacific*, Vol. 49, August 1937, 224.

20. Beals, C.S. and Blanchet, G.H. "An absorption line at λ 4430.6 of possibly interstellar origin, in *Monthly Notices of the Royal Astronomical Society*, Vol. 98, March 1938, 398.

21. Blanchet, Guy, "In the Land of the Muskox," in *Canadian Geographic Journal*, Vol. 8, #6, June 1934, 249–58; "The Caribou of the Barren Ground," in *The Beaver*, Vol. 16, #2, Sept. 1936; "The Last of

the Brigades," in *The Beaver*, Vol. 17, #4, March 1938; "Pioneer Surveys," in *The Beaver*, Vol. 18, #2, Sept. 1938; "Conquering the Northern Air," in *The Beaver*, Vol. 18 #4, March 1939.

22.   Harper, W.E., "Notes and Queries" in *Journal of the Royal Astronomical Society of Canada*, Vol. 33, 29.

Chapter 9: Strange Interlude: 1939–1941

1.   List or Manifest of Alien Passengers for the United States, #8 and #17.
2.   BCA, MS-0498, box 5, notebooks and diaries, 1939.
3.   BCA, MS-0498, box 10. While the gist of this chapter is based on Blanchet's memoir, it also draws heavily on his diary from box 5.
4.   Wright, Ronald, *On Fiji Islands* (New York: Viking, 1986) 84–88.
5.   Ibid, 150.
6.   "The old lady, while stroking my bare arm. told me that she had tried to cook part of a Missionary; she had boiled it for three days and it was still tough. It was a leg and she said perhps the boot was still on." This is a subtle reminder of the missionary Thomas Baker, who was eaten in 1867. As a result, the Wesleyan Church taught the following song to Mission children:

> Oh! dead is Mr. Baker
> They killed him on the road,
> And they ate him, boot and all.

Taken from Ronald Wright, *On the Islands of Fiji*, 86
7.   BCA, MS-0498, box 1, #4, letters from New Zealand.
8.   Letter from George Douglas to P.G. Downes, Feb. 8, 1943, courtesy of Enid Mallory.
9.   BCA, MS-0498, box 5, notebooks and diaries, 1948. Thomson, Vol. 3, 163–65.
10.   Thomson, Vol.3, 163–65.
11.   Berton, 113, and 565, 566.
12.   Prentice G. Downes was an American schoolteacher who had a penchant for the Canadian wilderness. In 1932, he went north on the Mackenzie River to Great Bear Lake, and on his return from Yellowknife to Fort Resolution on a barge, he met one of his heroes — George Douglas, the author of *Lands Forlorn*, one of his most prized books. A great friendship developed between the two men. In his travels later in the 1930s, Downes enjoyed getting up to the Barrens by going up Reindeer Lake and exploring the little-travelled area around Kasba Lake and the Kazan River. He relished his contacts with the Chipewyan people and they have a prominent place in his one book, *Sleeping Island*.
13.   Letter from George Douglas, see note #8.
14.   NAC, RG24. The Army Discharge certificate and Service and Casualty

form indicate that Blanchet was hospitalized in England, Oct. 22, 1941, and honourably discharged in Vancouver on Dec. 31, 1941.

Chapter 10: The Canol Project: 1942

1. Information from Cathy Converse, biographer of Capi Blanchet.
2. Barry, P.S., *The Canol Project: An Adventure of the U.S. War Department in Canada's Northwest* (Edmonton: s.n., 1984) 9.
3. Richard Finnie, "The Origin of Canol's Mackenzie Air Fields," in *Arctic*, Vol. 33, #2, June, 1980, 273–79.
4. Ibid, 276.
5. Don W. Thomson, "Oil over the Mountains," in *North*, May-June, 1970, edited posthumously from Blanchet's Canol diaries, 14–23; 38–44.
6. Ibid.
7. Barry, 159–61.
8. Don W. Thomson, see Note 5.
9. Watt, Frederic B., *Great Bear: A Journey Remembered* (Yellowknife: Outcrop Ltd., 1980) 76–77.

Chapter 11: Canol Continues: 1943–1944

1. Don W. Thomson, "Oil over the Mountains," in *North*, May–June, 1970.
2. BCA, MS-0498, box 4, diaries 1942–43; letter to the author from Eileen, (Mrs. Peter) Blanchet, April 14, 2002.
3. BCA, MS-0498, box 4.
4. Guy Blanchet, "Pack Train Reconnaissance of the Pipeline Route," unpublished typescript, Archives, Glenbow Alberta Institute, Calgary, 1–19.
5. Barry, 450-51; "Pack Train Reconnaissance," 10–11.
6. BCA, MS-0498, box 4, April 1943.
7. BCA, MS-0498, box 17, #3, "Canol," a saga by C.C. Wilcox.
8. Gage, S. R., *A Walk on the Canol Road: Exploring the First Major Northern Pipeline* (Oakville, ON: Mosaic Press, 1990) 64–69.
9. BCA, MS-0498, box 4.

Chapter 12: Final Working Years: 1944–1954

1. BCA, MS-0498, box 1.
2. Les Faulkner, "Summer Job Adventures for a Young Edmonton Student," in *Three Northern Wartime Projects*, (Bob Hesketh ed.) (Edmonton: Canadian Circumpolar Institute, and Edmonton and District Historical Society, 1966) 229–249.
3. BCA, MS-0498, box 1.
4. Letter from Max Cameron to Guy Blanchet, Sept. 30, 1948, from discarded correspondence files, Dept. of Energy, Mines and Resources, courtesy of Prof. R.H. Cockburn.

5. The examination was on the property laws of British Columbia, and Blanchet became a BCLS on April 10, 1945, e-mail, British Columbia Land Surveyors Association (BCLSA), May 6, 2007.

6. Webb, John Hooper, *The Big Inch: Surveying the TransMountain Pipeline, 1951-1952*. Saskatoon: J.H. Webb, 1993 ; Wilson, Neill C. and Frank J. Taylor, *The Building of Trans Mountain* (Vancouver: Trans Mountain Oil Pipe Line Company, 1954).

7. BCA, MS-0498, box 1, file #3, Trans Mountain pipeline correspondence.

8. Ibid.

9. Sandford, Barrie, *McCulloch's Wonder: The Story of the Kettle Valley Railway* (Vancouver: Whitecap Books, 1988) 160, 238.

10. BCA, MS-0498, box 1, file #3.

11. Wilson, Neill C. and Frank J. Taylor, *The Building of Trans Mountain* (Vancouver: Trans Mountain Oil Pipe Line Company, 1954) 14.

12. BCA, MS-0498, box 1, file #3.

13. Webb, John Hooper, 21.

14. Wilson, 43.

15. BCA, MS-0498, box 1, file #3.

Chapter 13: Writing, Friendship, Travel: 1954–1966

1. Personal information from Janet Blanchet.

2. BCA, MS-0498, box 10, 152–4.

3. Blanchet, review, *The Beaver*, Spring, 1956, 30.

4. NAC, MG-30 B95, Vol. 2, file #11, letter from George Douglas to Guy Blanchet, March 31, 1954.

5. Blanchet, review, *The Beaver*, Spring 1963, 58.

6. NAC, MG-30 B95, vol. 2, file #11, letter from George Douglas to Clifford Wilson, editor of *The Beaver*, Aug. 4, 1958.

7. *Canadian Literature*, Autumn, 1960, 84-85; *The Beaver*, Autumn 1960, 54.

8. BCA, MS-0498, box 15

9. NAC, MG-31 C6, Vol. 19, file #8, letter from Guy Blanchet to Richard Finnie, June 8, 1959.

10. Ibid, Blanchet to Finnie, Dec. 19, 1964.

11. Ibid, Blanchet to Finnie, Feb. 6, 1966.

12. Ibid, Eileen (Mrs. Guy) Blanchet to Finnie, Dec. 10, 1967, in response to a Christmas card: "Last year I had not the heart to write and tell you about Guy, and I hoped you would hear in some other way."

13. Conversation with Ingrid Blanchet, in Vancouver, April 2002.

Bibliography

Barry, P.S., *The Canol Project: An Adventure of the U.S. War Department in Canada's Northwest*. Edmonton: s.n., 1985.

Berton, Pierre, *Vimy*. Toronto: McClelland & Stewart, 1986.

Blanchet, Guy, *Aerial Mineral Exploration in Northern Canada*. Ottawa: King's Printer, 1930.

_____, *Great Slave Lake Area Northwest Territories*. Ottawa: King's Printer, 1926.

_____, *Search in the North*. Toronto: Macmillan, 1960.

Blondin, George, *Yamoria, the Lawmaker: Stories of the Dene*. Edmonton: NeWest Press, 1997.

Bond, Courtney, *City on the Ottawa*. Ottawa: Queen's Printer, 1961

_____, *Surveyors of Canada, 1867-1967*. Ottawa: Canadian Institute of Surveying, 1966.

Brown, Robert Craig and Ramsay Cook, *Canada 1896-1921: A Nation Transformed*. Toronto: McClelland & Stewart, 1974.

Christian, Edgar, George Whalley ed., *Death in the Barren Ground*. Ottawa: Oberon Press, 1980.

Douglas, George, *Lands Forlorn*. New York: Knickerbocker Press, 1914.

Eggleston, Wilfrid, *The Queen's Choice: A Story of Canada's Capital*. Ottawa: Queen's Printer, 1961.

Finkelstein, Max and James Stone, *Paddling the Boreal Forest: Rediscovering A.P. Low*. Toronto: Natural Heritage, 2004.

Finnie, Richard, *Canada Moves North*. New York: Macmillan, 1942.

Gage, S.R., *A Walk on the Canol Road : Exploring the First Major Northern Pipeline*. Oakville, ON: Mosaic Press, 1990.

Hodgins, Bruce and Gwyneth Hoyle, *Canoeing North into the Unknown: A Record of River Travel, 1874–1974*. Toronto: Natural Heritage Books, 1994.

LeBourdais, D.M., *Metals and Men: The Story of Canadian Mining*. Toronto: McClelland & Stewart, 1957.

MacGregor, J.G., *Vision of an Ordered Land: The Story of the Dominion Land Survey*. Saskatoon: Western Producer Prairie Books, 1981.

Main, J.R.K., *Voyageurs of the Air: A History of Civil Aviation in Canada, 1859-1967*. Ottawa: Department of Transport, Queen's Printer, 1967.

Mallory, Enid, *Coppermine: The Far North of George M. Douglas.* Peterborough: Broadview Press Ltd., 1989.

Molson, K.M., *Pioneering in Canadian Air Transport.* Winnipeg: James Richardson & Sons Limited, 1974.

Morse, Eric W., *Freshwater Saga: Memoirs of a Lifetime of Wilderness Canoeing in Canada.* Toronto: University of Toronto Press, 1987.

Pearce, Richard, *Marooned in the Arctic: Diary of the Dominion Explorers' Expedition to the Arctic.* Toronto: s.n., 1931. Richard Pearce was editor of *The Northern Miner.*

Sanford, Barrie, *McCulloch's Wonder: The Story of the Kettle Valley Railway.* Vancouver: Whitecap Books, 1978, 1988.

Seton, Ernest Thompson, *The Arctic Prairies: A Canoe-journey of 2,000 Miles in Search of the Caribou; Being the Account of a Voyage to the Region North of Aylmer Lake.* New York: Harper and Row, 1911, 1981.

Shackleton, Kathleen, *Arctic Pilot: Life and Work on North Canadian Air Routes, the experiences of Walter E. Gilbert, as told to Kathleen Shackleton.* Toronto: Thomas Nelson and Sons, 1940.

Shaw, Margaret Mason, *Bush Pilots.* Toronto: Clarke, Irwin & Co., 1962.

Smith, Philip, *Harvest from the Rock: A History of Mining in Ontario.* Toronto: Macmillan of Canada, 1986.

Sutherland, Alice Gibson, *Canada's Aviation Pioneers: 50 Years of McKee Trophy Winners.* Toronto: McGraw-Hill Ryerson, 1978.

Thomson, Don W., *Men and Meridians: The History of Surveying and Mapping in Canada,* Vol.1, up to 1867; Vol. 2, 1867–1917; Vol. 3, 1917-1947. Ottawa: Queen's Printer, 1969.

Waldron, Malcolm, *Snow Man: John Hornby in the Barren Lands.* Montreal and Kingston: McGill-Queen's University Press, 1997.

Watt, Frederick B., *Great Bear: A Journey Remembered.* Yellowknife: Outcrop Ltd., 1980.

Webb, John Hooper, *The Big Inch: Surveying Trans Mountain Pipe Line.* Saskatoon: J.H. Webb, 1993.

Whalley, George, *The Legend of John Hornby.* Toronto: Macmillan, 1962, Laurentian Library, 1977.

Wilson, Neill C. and Frank J. Taylor, *The Building of Trans Mountain.* Vancouver: Trans Mountain Oil Pipe Line Company, 1954.

Woods, Shirley, *Ottawa, The Capital of Canada.* Toronto: Doubleday, 1980.

Wright, Ronald, *On Fiji Islands.* New York: Viking, 1986

Index